HALLOWEEN

O
O
O

HALL

HALLOWEEN

Copyright © 2001 by Martha Stewart Living Omnimedia, Inc.
11 West 42nd Street, New York, New York 10036
www.marthastewart.com

Originally published in book form by Martha Stewart
Living Omnimedia, Inc. in 2001. Published simultaneously
by Clarkson Potter/Publishers, Oxmoor House, Inc., and
Leisure Arts.

A portion of this work was previously published in
MARTHA STEWART LIVING.

Published by Clarkson Potter/Publishers,
New York, New York.
Member of the Crown Publishing Group.

Random House, Inc.
New York, Toronto, London, Sydney, Auckland
www.randomhouse.com

CLARKSON N. POTTER is a trademark and POTTER and
colophon are registered trademarks of Random House, Inc.

Printed in the United States of America.

Library of Congress Cataloging-in-Publication Data
Halloween: the best of Martha Stewart Living/by the
editors of Martha Stewart Living.—1st ed.
    1. Halloween decorations. 2. Handicraft.
    3. Halloween cookery. I. Martha Stewart Living.
TT900.H32 Hs45 2001
745.594'1646—dc21   2001021327

ISBN 0-609-80863-X

10 9 8 7 6 5 4 3 2 1

First Edition

CONTENTS

ALONG WITH ITS FELLOW *nocturnal creatures the bat and the cat, the great horned owl is one of the most familiar and time-honored symbols of Halloween in North America. This species' Latin name is Bubo virginianus, for Virginia, where it was first sighted by scientists. For its size— at least eighteen and a half to twenty-five inches high and three to four pounds in weight—this owl is one of the strongest birds on the planet.*

*e*VERY OCTOBER 31, AMERICANS JOIN TOGETHER TO TRY TO SCARE THE DAYLIGHTS OUT OF ONE ANOTHER. The thrill of a good scare is nothing new to the human race; nor is Halloween a newcomer on our calendars. Its marriage of fear and jubilation has kept it a vibrant holiday for more than two thousand years.

The world had plenty to fear back when the Celts of northern Europe held the first festival of Samhain. Pronounced "SOW-in," the word means "end of summer"; since the Celts recognized only two seasons, Samhain also marked the start of winter, and the festival celebrated both the harvest and the Celtic New Year. This was the one night when the veil between the living and the dead was believed to be most permeable. People anxious about what the future might hold performed divination spells, which were thought to be at their most powerful when spirits roamed the earth.

It must have been deeply unnerving to wait for spirits to manifest, because Samhain also inspired a clever means of self-preservation: camouflage. Throughout the land, people dressed up as ghouls and ghosts to blend in with the real ones, and then led parades out of town in the hope of luring evil spirits away. Meanwhile, Druid priests built elaborate hilltop bonfires to encourage the sun to return at the end of winter; for good fortune, families would rebuild the fires in their hearths with embers from a Druid's fire, which they carried home in hollowed-out turnips. To fend off any spirit that might interfere with their safe journey home, they carved scary faces into their turnips—these were the first jack-o'-lanterns.

In the Middle Ages, the Roman Catholic Church competed with Samhain by launching a trio of Christian holidays called Hallowmas—October 31 became All Hallows' Eve (later shortened to Halloween), November 1 became All Saints' Day, and November 2 was named All Souls' Day to honor nonsaints. Rather than set out treats for the dead, the faithful were now encouraged to offer "soul cakes" to the poor for their prayers on behalf of departed family members. Villagers dressed up as angels or devils and visited from house to house, an entertainment that evolved into trick-or-treating. Ironically, the Christian plan to subvert Samhain codified the holiday instead; Halloween remained the night of Hallowmas that was least associated with religion—just right for universal appeal in the diversely populated United States.

Still, Halloween's association with Catholicism meant it didn't travel well to all the American colonies. It took many years before fall festivals began to hint at what was to come, with ritual ghost stories, apple bobbing, and pranks. Each new immigrant group lent its own folklore to the celebrations. With the nineteenth century's huge influx of Irish and Scottish immigrants, America was ripe for Halloween to take hold.

Victorian America saw Halloween as a terrific excuse to throw a theme party. The popular press, finding good copy in the quaint superstitions of the past, spread the holiday across the nation. Divination, jack-o'-lantern carving, and all manner of Halloween and harvest-inspired games were the rage, and parties competed with the sport of mischief-making. Eventually, Halloween parties fell out of fashion with young adults, leaving the holiday to its rightful heirs: children. Trick-or-treating—a phrase that nods to the mischief promised if a masquerading visitor was not adequately "treated"—became a national pastime.

Remarkably, Halloween today creates a communion of spirits not unlike that of the ancient Celts. Every year, history adds new characters to the cast of beings trick-or-treaters bring to life; a local Halloween parade might feature Julius Caesar and Prince, zombies and Rugrats. But modern Halloween also has something else in common with the ancient Samhain: We face head-on what we find scariest, because maybe together, if we can embrace our fears, we can conquer them once and for all.

boo

LIGHTING THE NIGHT | CONJURING A GLOW | TRADING FACES | HAUNTING A HOUSE

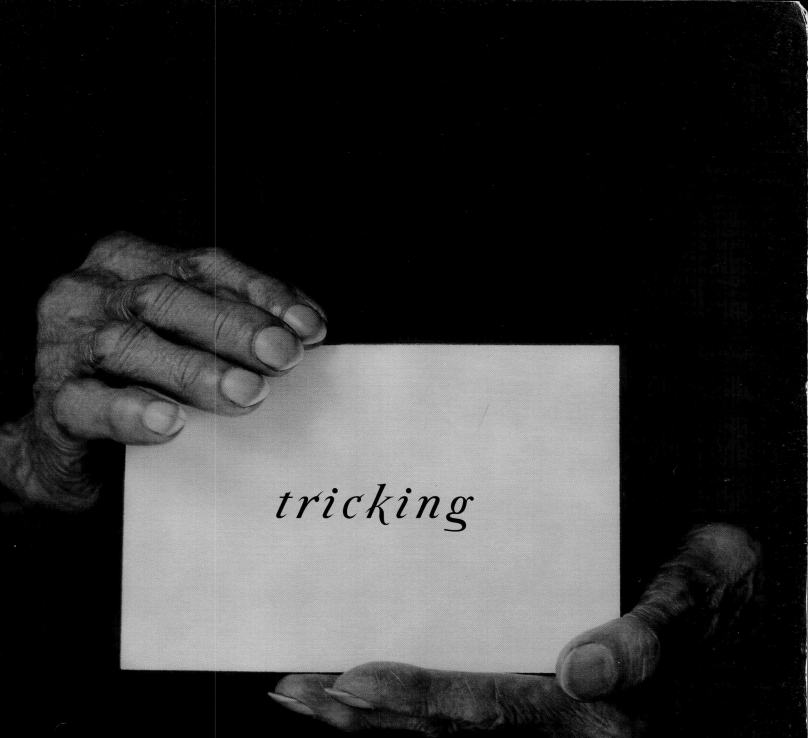

{ *LIGHTING THE NIGHT* }

*t*HE EXCITEMENT OF ALL HALLOW'S EVE IS
IN THE ETHER, THE ATMOSPHERE CHARGED
BY THE SIGHTS AND SOUNDS AND FEARS BELONGING
to the night—silhouetted trees groaning in the wind, bats whipping
overhead, fire-eyed cats jumping up from nowhere, witches chanting
around a bonfire. In the best scenario, there's a buttery harvest
moon, too, the closest we can come to a sun at midnight. And, every-
where, jack-o'-lanterns stand guard.

Capering fire and candlelight have accompanied nighttime activ-
ities for at least five thousand years, relied upon by humans to repel
the possible evil lurking in the dark as much as to light a way through
it. Candle glow seems all out of proportion with the size of the
flame—a single candle can illuminate a cave or living room well
enough to cause genuine wonder, like a lone soldier holding off
an invading army. Such is the trust we still invest in the power of
the ancient character Jack-O'-Lantern, whose light both dispels the
gloom and disperses tricksters at large.

Our most familiar Halloween symbol, the carved pumpkin has its
origins in the story of one particular Irish reveler. An unrepentant,
too-clever drunkard who twice made a soul-surrendering pact with
the devil—and twice tricked him into releasing his claim—Jack
met with the ultimate bad luck when he died. As a sinner, he could

ACCOMPANIED *by un-
decorated brethren, a horde
of carved pumpkins and
squash gathers on the porch
of this frame house. Some
are menacing, some merely
exasperated, some laugh
at a joke only a jack-o'-
lantern can hear. Together
they provide a dancing
patterned light to inform
demons, looking for a house
to haunt, that this one is
well guarded. All pumpkins
are safely lit with strings of
white outdoor lights.*

1 'NEW ENGLAND PIE'
  (SMALL SUGAR)
2 'ROUGE VIF D'ETAMPES'
  (CINDERELLA)
3 'ORANGE HOKKAIDO'
4 'GREEN HOKKAIDO'
5 'BLUE KABOCHA'
6 'RED TURBAN'
7 'LITTLE GEM HUBBARD'
8 'SWEETMEAT'
9 'GOLD NUGGET'
10 'GREEN KABOCHA'
11 'MUNCHKIN'
12 'LITTLE BOO'
13 'JACK BE LITTLE'

not be admitted to heaven, and, with perhaps not enough malice aforethought, he had also surrendered his passport to hell. The devil, in a rare moment of pity and grudging respect, cast him a single coal from the inferno. Placed in a hollowed-out turnip, it lit his way through relentless limbo.

Doomed to wander, Jack eventually crossed the Atlantic, and in America his glowing coal found a spacious new home in the corpulent native pumpkins, which provided him a larger canvas for self-expression. The pumpkins in these pages venture far beyond the traditional sneering, snaggle-toothed jack-o'-lantern face. We think Jack would approve of bringing a sculptor's eye to the task of pumpkin carving. Take inspiration from portraits by Matisse or Klee or Picasso, from eighteenth-century silhouettes or the Elgin Marbles or the Sistine Chapel. You might also look to the natural world for ideas; carve Jack's lantern a face of moon and stars, fallen leaves, nocturnal critters. Give it patterns harlequin diamonds, polka dots, spirals (ancient symbols of worlds in motion), and starbursts.

Don't limit yourself to pumpkins and candles; explore the potential of paper and electricity, too. Inscribe paper-bag luminarias along a back stair with an advisory rebus: *I'd turn back if [eye] were U.* Lay a path to your door with carved pumpkins positioned over the bulbs on a string of lights; riddle a pumpkin with holes, and fill each one with a spiky bulb. What we're after is to beat the holiday's phosphorescent spirits at their own game, to dispel their threat using the same palette of darting amber and inky shadow they use to scare us.

choosing a pumpkin

The squash family (all pumpkins and gourds are properly referred to as squash) encompasses hundreds of varieties in a motley parade of shapes and colors: bright-orange 'Rouge Vif d'Etampe' (also called Cinderella); 'Green Kabocha'; sugary 'Red Turban' and tiny 'Gold Nugget'; pallid, moon-shaped 'Lumina'; the traditional-orange 'Atlantic Giant' (opposite). Any and all are ripe for carving. Seek out the appropriately named 'Little Boo' and his equally charming and inedible friends, 'Jack Be Little' and 'Munchkin.' The spirits behind the squeezed faces cut into miniature squashes glare with particular ferocity.

ONCE LITTLE MORE THAN *freaks at agricultural fairs, giant pumpkins continue to grow in popularity. They need a lot of room to grow—seedlings are planted at least twenty feet apart. As they approach full size, they can gain ten to twenty pounds per day. Some champion growers feed their pumpkins milk.*

JACK-O'-LANTERNS *seem to have risen from the grave as Halloween night arrives in the cemetery. A single eyeball carved into the small pie squash perched atop a headstone keeps a watchful eye on the gathering throng. Blue, white, and green varieties augment the more familiar army of chubby orange field pumpkins. A wide net was cast for designs, too: wizards' stars and moons, suns and swirls and tumbling waves, grinning demons and winsome abstract portraits.*

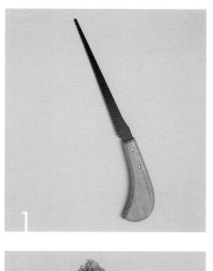
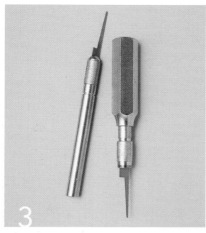

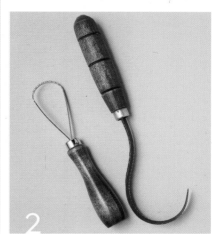

basic pumpkin carving

None of the tools above was made for carving pumpkins, but each is invaluable in the process of fashioning original Halloween characters, such as the bemused fellow at left. Let the squash itself be your guide to the personality within. Will he need one eye or two? Be laughing or scowling? While some fancy julienning elevates better kitchens, pumpkin carving summons the Michelangelo in us all. **1.** A small saw is ideal for piercing a hard pumpkin shell; the flexible blade makes circular cuts easy. Use it to make large openings at top, back, or bottom. **2.** Tools for scraping and molding, such as this large scraper (with loop) and fleshing tool (with hook), come in many sizes and are great for removing pulp and thinning the walls of a pumpkin. **3.** Thin, sturdy miniature saws make irregular cutting easier.

A GOLD-LIT *lane (opposite) is made from two strings of outdoor-safe electric carnival lights and 'Lumina' pumpkins. Pine needles hide the utility cords (but they should be brushed away from bulbs).* RIGHT: *Cut a hole in the base of each pumpkin; remove seeds and flesh. Hammer a small cookie or canapé cutter into the skin in a regular pattern. Remove cutters with pliers; finish holes with a thin serrated knife. Position a pumpkin over each bulb.*

pumpkin-punching tools

Thick-skinned pumpkins can be tricky to carve with a knife, but certain tools make the job easier. **1.** Hole cutters, available at hardware stores, are short pipes with sharp ends, one angled end and one capped. They can be pressed through the toughest shells to make perfect holes. Using two sizes of hole cutters creates a random, bubbled effect. **2.** Straight out of your kitchen drawers, metal cookie cutters come in handy for various nonhuman shapes—stars, diamonds, and small animals. For the most efficient handling, use a kitchen mallet or small hammer to tap cutters into the shell, as was done to produce a selection of star-shape holes in this field pumpkin.

ADD TWINKLE *to the darkest fall nights with a galaxy of pumpkin lanterns (opposite and right). Drill constellations of tiny holes into each pumpkin with hole cutters and a power drill; experiment with different random and geometric designs. Try a real constellation, too, if you dare.*

celestial pumpkins

YOU WILL NEED PUMPKINS | SAW OR CARVING KNIFE | SCRAPER | POWER DRILL AND ONE-QUARTER-INCH BIT | WHITE CHRISTMAS LIGHTS

First, lay a pumpkin on its side and use a saw or knife to carve out a circular hole in the bottom, large enough for your hand to fit comfortably through. Remove flesh and seeds. With a scraper, scrape away pumpkin's inner wall until it is about one-quarter inch thick. Turn pumpkin right side up. **1.** Fit a power drill with a bit. **2.** Drill holes at random across the shell, or follow a uniform pattern that you have laid out with tape. **3.** Insert a string of white or clear lights through the bottom opening, and push one bulb through each hole so that all bulbs extend beyond the pumpkin shell. Bind remaining lights inside the pumpkin so they don't touch the rind. Turn pumpkin right side up with plug running out from the bottom.

STRUNG FROM *the rafters of a porch, electric jack-o'-lanterns supply an original outdoor-lighting solution for Halloween or autumn entertaining. This hanging garden of unearthly delights (opposite) is made of brightly dressed decorative gourds dispersed along a string of utility lights. Each wears a patterned coat made with a power drill.*

gourd lanterns

YOU WILL NEED SMALL GOURDS | UTILITY KNIFE AND SAW BLADE | POWER DRILL AND ONE-QUARTER-INCH BIT | DOUBLE-ENDED SCULPTING TOOL | STRING OF UTILITY LIGHTS

Autumn's decorative gourds find life beyond the centerpiece as hanging outdoor lights. Gourd flesh is very hard. Fit a utility knife with a saw blade and power drill with a bit. **1.** To make a hole in the gourd's base wide enough for a utility lightbulb socket, drill small holes close together. Connect the dots to cut out a circular hole. Repeat the process at the top, but make only two or three small drill holes; the opening at the top must be sized to grip the bulb socket inserted into each lantern. **2.** Hollow out the gourd with the sculpting tool (available at hardware or art stores). **3.** Drill holes in the shell in a decorative pattern. Push bulb sockets into top, smaller hole; screw lightbulb into it from inside the gourd. **4.** Use utility lights with sockets that are prespaced along a wire, or space them yourself along zip cord wire using carnival light-socket fixtures (available at lighting-supply stores).

Will you join us on the Eve
When Jack-o'-lanterns flare?
Ghosts and witches all insist
That-you-be-there!

apple votives

YOU WILL NEED APPLES | WASHTUB OR OTHER LARGE
TUB | TEA LIGHTS | UTILITY KNIFE | LEMONS

For gently bobbing apple candleholders, first toss
whole apples into a tub of water. Each will float differ-
ently; mark their topsides with one dot apiece, and
remove from water. Centering the bottom of a tea
light over the dot, trace the candle's circumference
onto the apple skin, then cut out the circle with a utility knife inserted as deep as the candle is tall. Hollow
out apple with a spoon so the top of the tea light will
be flush with the fruit's surface. Squeeze lemon juice
onto the cut fruit to prevent browning; insert candle,
and light. Keep a flotilla bobbing by the door.

THE LOW WATTAGE *from standard large-bulb carnival lights provides a safe source of illumination for carved lanterns, particularly for small fellows like these multifarious squash and gourds. Make watchtowers of groups of three and four mismatched squash; give their faces a range of expressions. Line them up along a stone wall, and they will look as though they can spot any approaching spooks from a long way off.*

leafy pumpkins

YOU WILL NEED FALLEN LEAVES | PREPARED PUMPKINS | LINOLEUM CUTTER | CANDLES OR UTILITY LIGHTS

The autumn leaves carved into these woodsy jack-o'-lanterns retain their daytime glow. Fallen leaves are the only templates you will need. **1.** Tape leaves to a cleaned pumpkin shell with the top cut out, and outline them with a pencil. **2.** Use a linoleum cutter with a narrow blade to peel away the rind and expose the flesh. Carve decorative motifs or realistic "veins" in the leaf; go as deep as possible without puncturing flesh, especially if you will be lighting the pumpkin with candles. **3.** Another option is to cut out the entire leaf shape with a utility knife, remove it, and carve patterns into it with a long utility knife. Then reposition the chunky leaf, letting it protrude slightly. The pumpkins on this porch are lit with forty-watt bulbs: Use utility-light sockets that come attached to a cord approved for outdoor use. Cut a hole in the rear of the pumpkin to slip cord through. You will need several candles to get bright enough light for a pumpkin carved with a linoleum cutter. Cut another hole, at the top rear of the pumpkin, for ventilation.

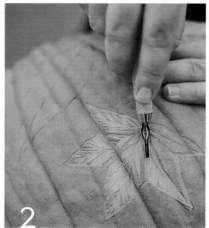

A MONOGRAMMED pumpkin filled with branches of bittersweet and pear leaves (below) stands beside the door to Martha's house. A waxed-paper "curtain" tacked inside the pumpkin softens the glare of electric lights. Another way to apply a monogram is to pare away only half the pumpkin flesh, rather than carving all the way through, to produce a muted glow.

monogramming pumpkins

YOU WILL NEED MONOGRAM TEMPLATE | PHOTOCOPIER | PUMPKIN | CARVING KNIFE | NEEDLE TOOL | HOLE CUTTER | SABER SAW | LINOLEUM CUTTER | CHRISTMAS LIGHTS | SMALL GLASS | WAXED PAPER

If you really want the world to know which pumpkin you carved, why not personalize it with a monogram? Photocopy a monogram you have drawn or put together from photocopies of letters you like. Enlarge to a size appropriate for your pumpkin. Prepare the pumpkin by removing seeds and flesh, and cutting a large hole in the bottom with a carving knife. **1.** Tape monogram template to the pumpkin. Using a needle tool (available at hardware stores), poke holes at close intervals around each letter, carefully marking corners. Remove the photocopy, and connect the needle-tool dots with a pen. Use a hole cutter to make the first opening in a letter, then a saber saw to cut along the pen lines; a linoleum cutter will help cut into tight corners. Cut all the way through. **2.** Wrap Christmas lights around a glass to make a radiant light source. Even out the light by tacking a sheet of waxed paper over the inside of the monogram. Position pumpkin over glass.

A SILENT *"boo" issues from a paper-bag lantern (left).* OPPOSITE: *The letters for this ascending warning were set in old-fashioned type on a computer, enlarged on a photocopier, and cut out with a utility knife. Votive candles in glass jars provide the flickering light.*

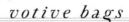

votive bags

YOU WILL NEED PAPER BAGS | STENCILS | UTILITY KNIFE | CARDBOARD | GLUE STICK | CANDLES IN GLASSES | LIGHTER

Plain brown-paper bags spell danger for arriving tricksters. The softly lit scare tactics are simple to employ. You need two same-sized bags for each lantern. **1.** Using stencils, outline letters, phrases, or designs on one bag; cut out with a utility knife. Insert a piece of cardboard in between the two sides of the bag to avoid cutting through both of them. Do not discard center cutouts from letters with closed shapes, such as A or O. **2.** Fold top edge of second bag over twice. Trim top of stenciled bag so that it is slightly shorter than the bag with folded edge. Run a glue stick around the edges of letters on the inside of the bag. Place folded bag inside cutout bag, tucking the stenciled bag under the folded edge of its companion. Press bags together; reposition any saved center cutouts, and glue to inside bag. To illuminate, hold a candle in its glass, halfway down into bag. Light with a lighter, and lower carefully.

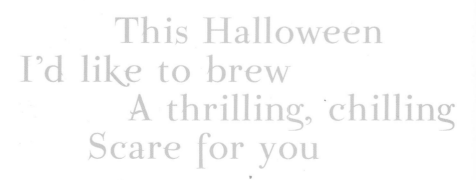

This Halloween
I'd like to brew
A thrilling, chilling
Scare for you

*O*F COURSE WE HAVE ABSOLUTELY NOTHING AGAINST JACK-O'-LANTERN: HIS CROOKED SMILE AND MENACING EYES ARE WELCOME ON ANY PORCH every October 31. But Jack has an alter ego, and that's the kind of squash you invite indoors.

Something happens when you light a pumpkin and suspend it in midair: When it no longer has to balance on its slightly lopsided bottom, its imperfections fade away, and it takes on an unexpected grace. Pumpkins made into temporary light fixtures can create an eerie but sophisticated atmosphere for your Halloween proceedings.

The chandeliers, lamps, and sconces in this chapter mimic the designs of classic light fixtures and show how well pumpkins lend themselves to that task. With pumpkins large and small you can fill windows with fiery, spiraling globes or hang over a dining table a lamp inspired by the art glass of Louis Comfort Tiffany. Small pumpkins make snug, sturdy holders for tea lights and votive candles. Using a grapevine wreath dressed with leaves and berries you can serve up a floating platter of small pumpkins that shimmers with the diffused warmth of opaque glass. Though some of these fixtures look intricate, all they really require are the proper tools and a bit of patience. Just allow time to do the project shortly before the holiday, since a carved pumpkin looks its best for only a day or two.

LIKE WORLDS *in orbit, a cluster of carved globes dangles from the ceiling on fine wire. The pumpkins are carved in spirals to reveal the shells at their thinnest, muting the candlelight so the orbs seem to glow by themselves. To keep them steady, always hang them from three evenly spaced wires joined together to make a hook or hanger at the top.*

The key to hanging pumpkins so they are balanced is to use three equally spaced suspending wires. If you desire more than three wires, use multiples of three to keep the fixture steady. Look for small, well-shaped pumpkins without any flat or discolored areas. Use a variety of tools for different effects—small serrated saws for cutting, and linoleum cutters and wood gouges for paring just the shell. Rub all cut areas with petroleum jelly to keep the pumpkins looking fresh as long as possible. Remember that candlelit pumpkins can become very hot, especially when coated with petroleum jelly. After snuffing the flames, let the lamps cool to room temperature before handling.

When lighting a house on Halloween, the overriding goal is to leave no corner unspooked. Any kind of light you can conjure up—whether inside a pumpkin or not—can be used to that end. Keep all lamps low and glowing. Consider casting beautiful beeswax candles in hollowed-out gourds to guard over tabletops. Line a staircase to a dark landing with votives burning in hollowed-out 'Crown-of-Thorns' squash. Adorn strings of white lights with conical shades in Halloween colors, giving each its

SOME OF THE containers that nature provides are as ingenious as anything a craftsman could dream up. The squash shells (opposite) in which these candles were molded are perfect examples. Stand the candles on pedestals of different shapes and heights to light a foyer or a Halloween party table.

own jack-o'-lantern smirk. Decorate glass votives and hurricanes with shuddering silhouettes.

Where there is spooky light there are spookier shadows; the air should be filled with them, as many as can invade a room. Shadow play will add dimension to the glowing half-light you have kindled throughout the house, lending a sense of heightened unreality: A shadow's very essence is movement and mystery; you cannot capture its chill and enchantment in a painting or photograph.

Unadorned paper lampshades make ideal screens for shadow play. Cutouts of bats and witches, ghosts and goblins hung inside a shade from various lengths of string will flutter at the slightest provocation, casting quivering shadows on the shade. To cast a shadow with a distinct outline, position the cutout close to the shade on which the shadow will be cast; the farther you remove it from the lightbulb, the more movement the shadow will have. As for the light itself, any brightness will do, but ideally you should decrease the wattage of the bulbs in your table lamps. On the holiday that celebrates darkness, it's best to wait until the morrow for a daylight kind of glare.

If you take a carrot on Hallowe'en night,
And, holding it over a candlelight,
Pinch your left ear, take off your left shoe,
This will mean good fortune to you.

molded squash candles

YOU WILL NEED ACORN SQUASH | SMALL KNIFE | MELON BALLER | WAX OR OLD CANDLES | CANDY THERMOMETER | WICKING | METAL WICK TABS

1. Remove squash stem and enough of top with a small knife to make an opening large enough for your hand. Remove seeds and loose pulp. Use melon baller to scoop out remaining pulp. Scrape top to bottom, along contours of squash for hollowed-out tunnels. Smooth lines between tunnels with spoon. **2.** Melt wax in metal pourer or saucepan set over, but not touching, a pot of boiling water, until a candy thermometer registers 180 degrees. Cut wicking three inches longer than squash is tall; attach metal wick tab to one end. Steady squash, if necessary, in a glass. Carefully pour wax into squash. Holding top of wick, drop metal tab into wax. Trim wick two inches above wax. **3.** Let sit until squash is cool, four to five hours. If center sinks during cooling, fill with more hot wax. When cooled, squash skin should peel away easily. To even bottom of candle, carve with a knife.

squash votive holders

YOU WILL NEED 'CROWN-OF-THORNS' SQUASH | SMALL KNIFE | MELON BALLER | VOTIVE CANDLES

To hollow out squash as candleholders to line a stairway (left), carve along their naturally jagged, seemingly collapsed tops. Remove seeds and pulp as for molded squash candles. Place glass votives inside squash.

hanging orbs

YOU WILL NEED PUMPKINS | SMALL KNIFE |
SCRAPER | WOOD GOUGE | PETROLEUM JELLY |
AWL | IRON WIRE | PLIERS | VOTIVE CANDLES

To make the hanging orbs that appear on page 30, choose well-shaped pumpkins of various sizes that are light enough so they will hang easily. With a small knife, cut off pumpkin tops; remove seeds. Scrape the interior walls with a scraper until flesh is no more than one inch thick. **1.** Using a wood gouge, cut a continuous spiral around the outside of each pumpkin, removing the rind so that light can shine through. Thinly coat exposed flesh with petroleum jelly.
2. Using an awl, punch three equally spaced holes near the edge of the opening, low enough so the pumpkin's weight will be supported. Thread iron wire through each hole, and knot with pliers to secure. Join the three wires so the pumpkin hangs evenly, making a loop at the top for a hanger. Insert votive candles, and hang at staggered heights.

GHOSTLY WHITE *pumpkins (above) are piled high on a porch, some mysteriously glowing. After a hole was cut in the bottom and the seeds and flesh were scooped out, the shells, like those used as hanging orbs, were carved with a wood gouge in continuous spirals from top to bottom, then placed over carnival lights.*

THREE PERFECTLY ROUND *pumpkin sconces—each made of two pumpkins—wear starburst aprons and jeweled crowns.* OPPOSITE: *A stately husband and wife seem hypnotized by the candle between their colonial-style silhouettes. The pumpkins were carved so that they could be displayed with their stems in opposing arabesques.*

pumpkin sconces

YOU WILL NEED FOR EACH SCONCE: TWO ROUND PUMP-KINS, ONE MEDIUM, THE OTHER ABOUT HALF AS BIG | SERRATED KNIFE | LINOLEUM CUTTER | VOTIVE CANDLES

1. Prepare the larger pumpkin by cutting a hole in its side with a serrated knife, and hollow it out until the shell is one-half inch thick. Using a small linoleum cutter, carve a shallow starburst design in the rind of the bottom surface of the pumpkin, but don't completely pierce the flesh. **2.** To help the pumpkin sit steadily on the shelf, create a flat surface by taking a small slice from the side opposite the opening. **3.** Cut off the bottom of the smaller pumpkin, and hollow out the shell to one-half inch thick. Remove the top of the pumpkin; create a decorative scalloped edge (see page 36) with a linoleum cutter. Set small pumpkin on top of the larger one so the two are balanced. TO ILLUMINATE: Lift off top pumpkin, set votive candles inside larger pumpkin, and light; carefully replace small pumpkin. You may need to cut a small hole in the back of the larger pumpkin for ventilation.

pumpkin silhouettes

YOU WILL NEED PHOTOGRAPHS OR CLIP ART | PERMANENT MARKER | PHOTOCOPIER | CORRECTION FLUID | PREPARED PUMPKINS | NEEDLE TOOL | LINOLEUM CUTTER | WOOD GOUGE | CANDLES OR LIGHTBULBS

Silhouettes can be made using standard photographs. You can also use clip-art books to find profiles. **1.** Snap the subject in profile, then color in the face, hair, and neck, as shown, with a permanent marker. Photocopy the darkened profile, and, if necessary, smooth lines around the back of the head with correction fluid. Draw an oval around the silhouette to create a cameo face. **2.** With the photocopy of the profile taped in place, outline the profile and the oval with a needle tool and pen. Remove the photocopy. **3.** Using a linoleum cutter in narrow places and a wood gouge in open areas, scoop out pumpkin flesh surrounding the holes and pen marks until you have a profile in silhouette. Place a candle or low-wattage lightbulb and socket inside the pumpkin to provide illumination.

tiffany-style lamp

YOU WILL NEED TWO ROUND PUMPKINS, ONE ABOUT THREE TIMES AS LARGE AS THE OTHER | MASKING TAPE | WOOD GOUGE | MALLET | LINOLEUM CUTTER | AWL | HEAVY TWINE | WOODEN SKEWERS | LIGHTBULB ON CORD

1. On larger pumpkin, mark a line with masking tape halfway up the shell—use a ruler to be sure height is same all around. With a large wood gouge, carefully pierce shell above tape, making scalloped cuts all around pumpkin, connecting each cut with the next. Use a mallet, if necessary, to knock tool all the way through shell. Split pumpkin in half, then hollow out bottom half to one-inch thickness. **2.** With linoleum cutter or wood gouge, carve oval cutouts, about one-quarter inch deep, beneath each scallop around top edge. **3.** Punch three holes through large pumpkin with an awl. Make holes equidistant, between scalloped edges where rind is intact, and low enough so that the weight of the pumpkin will be well supported. For hanger, wrap even lengths of heavy twine several times through each hole, and tie securely. **4.** Repeat steps 1 and 2 with smaller pumpkin, but make scalloped cuts about a third of the way down from top. Use a small linoleum cutter to make a starburst pattern in bottom of smaller pumpkin. Using the circumference of smaller pumpkin as a guide, cut a hole in bottom of larger pumpkin shell. Make scalloped cuts around its new edge. To assemble, stick sturdy wooden skewers through top of small pumpkin, forming an X, then lower smaller pumpkin through hole in larger one, letting it hang. Light with a bulb on a cord, the safest choice for this pumpkin fixture; candles won't balance well inside it.

INSPIRED BY *the work of Louis Comfort Tiffany, this elegant fixture (above) recalls the marvelous stained-glass lamps created by his studio. A lightbulb, a more vivid and practical light source than candles, illuminates the scalloped edges and starburst details.*

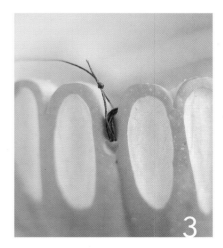
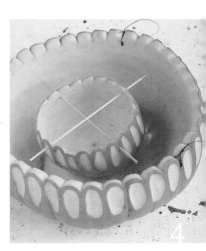

CASUALLY ADORNED *with colorful fallen leaves and autumn berries, a simple grapevine wreath (opposite) is illuminated by tea lights set inside miniature pumpkins. Suspend it from a ceiling hook to lend a welcoming light to a front window. To ensure that the glow will last through your party, wait until just before guests arrive to light candles.*

wreath lamp

YOU WILL NEED TEA LIGHTS | WAX PENCIL | SIX MINIATURE PUMPKINS | SMALL KNIFE OR SAW | SPOON OR FLESHING TOOL | BALL CHAIN | BRASS COUPLINGS | S HOOK | GRAPEVINE WREATH | FLORAL WIRE | AWL | WIRE CUTTERS | IRON WIRE | LEAVES | BERRIES

1. Using a tea light as a guide, trace a circle in wax pencil on top of six miniature pumpkins. Cut out the shape with a small knife or saw. Remove top, and scoop out insides with a spoon or fleshing tool. **2.** Make a hanger using three equal lengths of ball chain; attach brass couplings to the ends of each. Gather all three together, and slip an S hook through the holes in the couplings. Join the other ends to the grapevine wreath by passing floral wire through the coupling and winding it around wreath form, spacing them evenly along the periphery. **3.** With an awl, make two holes one inch apart through the bottom of each pumpkin. Bend an iron wire into a U shape, then thread it through holes from the inside. Wrap wire around wreath form, and twist underneath to secure. Decorate wreath with leaves and berries—these are pear, maple, and oak leaves, and bittersweet berries. Place tea lights inside pumpkins.

shadow lanterns

YOU WILL NEED HEAT-PROOF JARS OR GLASSES |
PHOTOCOPIER | ACETATE OR BLACK PAPER | TEA LIGHTS |
VELLUM | UTILITY KNIFE | DOUBLE-SIDED TAPE

1. We used cylindrical glass vases for our lanterns, but any straight-sided, heat-proof jar or glass will work. Enlarge the templates (see page 137) on a photocopier, or make your own designs. Copy designed page or pages onto sheets of acetate at a good copy shop (you can also simply cut shapes from black paper to tape to the outside of the glass). Tape the acetate around the vase. Place a tea light inside. **2.** Cut a piece of vellum with a utility knife for a sleeve to fit loosely around the vase. The sleeve should be about one inch taller than the vase and about one-half to three-quarters inch bigger than the vase all around. The elbowroom will give shadows more room to dance. Secure edges of vellum together with double-sided tape, and light candle.

SHADOWS TWITTER *across the surface of heat-proof vases surrounded with acetate photocopies of bats and spiders and other spooky forms. You can cut out shapes from black paper for a reverse effect. Consider other classic Halloween symbols, too, such as owls and witches. You can even tell a horror story—whose are those silhouettes in the windows?*

SURPRISE *guests or trick-or-treaters with a bat-filled lampshade. Inside the shade, black-paper cutouts are suspended from different lengths of white thread. The smallest vibration makes them flutter.*

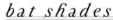

bat shades

YOU WILL NEED PHOTOCOPIER | WHITE PENCIL | BLACK PAPER | UTILITY KNIFE | PLAIN, LIGHT-COLORED LAMPSHADE | 20-GAUGE BRASS WIRE | WHITE THREAD | CLEAR REMOVABLE TAPE

1. Make a stencil by photocopying bat template on page 137. With a white pencil, trace shape several times onto black paper; cut out each shape with a utility knife. **2.** You'll need a white or light-colored lampshade made of translucent paper or styrene. To hang bats, use 20-gauge brass wire to make a ring that will fit just inside the top of the shade, resting on the spokes. Tape one end of a piece of white thread to the paper bat; tie the other to the ring. Hang bats at varying heights to mimic a swarm. Depending on the shape of the shade, bats near the bottom may not cast clear shadows. In that case, tape more bats directly to the inside of the shade with clear removable tape.

NOT EVERY *jack-o'-lantern has to be round or even lit with a candle. These ghoulish string-light lampshades (right) gleefully convey the Halloween spirit and stack easily when it's time to put them away.* OPPOSITE: *Fill your windowsill with a cackling crowd of hurricane lamps. They're less messy to make than carved pumpkins but every bit as menacing.*

jack-o'-lantern shades

YOU WILL NEED PROTRACTOR OR PLATE | GLOSSY TISSUE PAPER | STYRENE LAMPSHADE LINER | UTILITY KNIFE | STRING OF LIGHTS | HURRICANES | GERMAN TISSUE PAPER | WHITE PAPER | DOUBLE-SIDED TAPE | CANDLES

1. To make conical shades for a string of lights, use a protractor or an upside-down plate to draw semicircles on glossy tissue paper and on thick styrene lampshade liner (see the Guide), which resists heat. With the dimensions of the shade in mind, draw grinning faces or other designs onto the paper. Cut out designs with a utility knife, and lay tissue over styrene. Fold shade into a cone, and staple edges together; make sure the opening fits snugly over the lightbulb socket. Slip on the shade, then screw in the bulb. **2.** For hurricanes, measure the height and circumference of a cylindrical vase or hurricane votive holder. For each lantern, cut two rectangles of different-colored German tissue paper (see the Guide) to those dimensions. Draw a spooky face freehand on white paper, and lay it under a sheet of tissue. Cut out features with a utility knife. Wrap the other sheet of tissue around the candleholder, and secure it with double-sided tape. Do the same with the cutout sheet. Place a cinnamon or other scented candle inside for autumn spice.

*t*HE FACE GAZING BACK AT YOU IN THE MIR-ROR IS DRAWN AND PALE. YOUR EYES ARE LOST IN OMINOUS SHADOWS, AND YOUR LIPS ARE THE COLOR of blood. You look perfect. Every Halloween, beauty takes on a different meaning. With either makeup or a mask, you can become a more frightful or more fantastical version of yourself.

Makeup artist Tim Considine of Direct Effects in Los Angeles has made a career of giving ordinary faces shocking new looks. On these pages he demonstrates how to achieve remarkable effects with a few simple techniques. His classic vampire, skeleton, mummy, and cat, as well as Martha's bewitching Black Widow (for which he teamed up with makeup artist Hiromi Kobari), depend on makeup fundamentals such as shading and contouring, aging and texturizing the skin, and applying prosthetic features and facial hair. Make these faces your own, or adapt a technique or two to your costume.

Most of the makeup projects require basic supplies such as cream makeup or greasepaint, spirit gum or another adhesive, shadows, pencils, and powder. Before using any product, be sure you have the appropriate remover. Some substances can be washed off with soap and water; others call for special solvents.

Always apply makeup to a clean face for smooth, even applica-tion. Use a light touch. "Stop before you think you've done enough,"

MARTHA SHOWS *Hallo-ween makeup at its most glamorous and spine-tingling. Naturally, the Black Widow is always accompanied by her minions; these plastic spiders crawl all over her neck and face (with the assis-tance of a little spirit gum).*

Considine advises. "You can always go back and apply more, but it's a lot of work to remove makeup and start over." Whatever look you decide upon, never use an adhesive on your skin that isn't made for that purpose—or you may be, quite literally, stuck with your new face.

A painted face is a complete costume: A person in normal street clothes but sporting green skin and vampire teeth is more completely disguised than one in full Carmen Miranda regalia without lipstick and eyeliner. Masks have even more power. They are a means of transport into other bodies, minds, times, and places—a way to explore the unfathomable. From deepest time, people have worn masks to take on new identities, to appease or invoke gods and spirits, and to summon the noble qualities of wildlife—the eagle's daring, the lion's strength.

The masks shown here are all born in nature; we call them "bird mask," "leaf mask," and the like, but they are not really meant to "be" one thing or another. On Halloween you can be a feeling, a color,

MASK OR MAKEUP?
Nature provides inspiration, and even materials, for both. Greasepaints and powders (below left) are prized for achieving ghastly effects with makeup. Preserved leaves and petals (below right) transform plain party-store masks into faces from the fairy kingdom. Replace elastic bands with ribbons, and use craft glue to apply decorations. OPPOSITE: *This winsome matching cap and mask are decorated with vintage paper flower petals.*

a flower, or fall itself. Playful enough for trick-or-treating, yet sophisticated enough for an elegant Halloween ball, these masks work equally well with a sweater and jeans or a party dress.

Each began as a plain store-bought mask. There are just two tricks to dressing them up: Replace the elastic bands with lengths of shimmering ribbon, and cover the masks with beautiful things found in nature (or, if you prefer, some man-made replicas): overlapping layers of paper flowers, pressed maple leaves, vibrant hydrangea petals, dried fern fronds, polka-dotted guinea-hen feathers. Let the form of the materials dictate the designs.

Basic masks, which come in several shapes, are available at costume and novelty shops. Florists and craft stores carry everything else; for some truly exquisite embellishments, try a milliner's-supply store. And don't forget your own backyard.

flower mask and cap

YOU WILL NEED CRAFT GLUE | PAPER OR FABRIC FLOWER
PETALS | PLAIN MASK | BRIDAL CAP | WIRED PAPER
LEAVES | HOT GLUE GUN | THIN STICK OR BRANCH

Glue paper or fabric petals (available at craft stores)
to a mask and bridal cap (see the Guide). If petals are
soft and flexible, fold them around eyeholes and glue
to the back of mask; otherwise, glue on front of mask
so they frame the eyeholes to your liking. Twist stems
of several wired paper leaves (wire glued behind the
major vein) around a pencil or thin stick. Pull out pencil
with a flourish, creating a curlicue. Glue to the top
of cap for a crown. Use a hot glue gun to attach mask
to a stick or thin tree or shrub branch for a handle.

fern or leaf mask

YOU WILL NEED BROWN SPRAY PAINT | PLAIN MASK |
RIBBON | DRIED FERN FRONDS | SPRAY ADHESIVE | PRE-
SERVED LEAVES | PAINTBRUSH | CRAFT GLUE

1. For fern mask, spray-paint mask brown and replace
elastic with ribbon. Because the fronds are delicate,
apply a coat of spray adhesive instead of glue to the
fronds, and place them so that the stems are at the
nose and the tips come to a point beyond edge of mask.
2. For the leaf mask, let the velvety undersides of preserved leaves be on display. Replace elastic with ribbon.
Brush craft glue onto the front side of one leaf at a
time and position on mask, working from outside in. Fold
leaves through eyeholes, and glue to back of mask.

THIS RED OAK-LEAF *mask is devilish, and no wonder: A New England fable tells of an old man who tricked the devil into letting him live until the oak lost all its leaves. Oaks rarely do, and in anger, the hoodwinked devil chewed the leaves into their distinctive spiky shape. The silvery companion mask is heavenly, swept with bleached fern fronds as if touched by early frost. For ties, use silky ribbons—autumnal orange for the turned oak leaves and rich brown satin for the ferns.*

black widow

YOU WILL NEED EYEBROW PLASTIC | WHITE AND BLACK CREAM MAKEUP | FOAM SPONGE | NO-COLOR POWDER | MAKEUP BRUSHES | DARK-GREEN FROSTING POWDER | EYELASH ADHESIVE | FALSE EYELASHES | RED LIP LINER | RED LIPSTICK | POWDER BLUSH | HAIR GEL | BLACK WIG | PLASTIC SPIDERS | COTTON SWABS | SPIRIT GUM | BLACK GLUE-ON FINGERNAILS

MARTHA'S BLACK WIDOW WAS INSPIRED BY THE QUEEN OF THE SPIDERS IN ITALIAN MAKEUP ARTIST STEPHANO ANSELMO'S BOOK *IL TRUCCO E LA MASCHERA.*

1. Cover eyebrows: Soften a small amount of eyebrow plastic between fingers, then spread over the brow in the direction of hair growth. Cover with white cream makeup. With a sponge, apply a sheer layer of white cream makeup to face and neck; powder to set. **2.** With black cream makeup, paint high, arching eyebrows with small makeup brush; extend color up, at an angle, from inside corner of eyebrow, dramatically shading above brows. Add dark-green frosting powder for contouring; blend with sponge. **3.** Using a tiny makeup brush, apply a thin line of eyelash adhesive to back of false eyelashes; press into place along lash line of each eye. **4.** Using black cream makeup and an eyeliner brush, line each eye top and bottom, extending outward from corner of eye. **5.** With red lip liner, outline lips, shaping top lip into a sharp V at the center; fill in with red lipstick. **6.** With a fan-shaped brush, sweep powder blush out and down from corner of eye. A paper template can be useful in keeping shading even and contours symmetrical. **7.** Use gel to slick back hair; carefully fit on black wig. **8.** Attach plastic spiders to face: Use a cotton swab to dab spirit gum on back of spider, let dry until tacky, then press onto skin, holding in place for a moment or two. Finish with long black fingernails.

skeleton

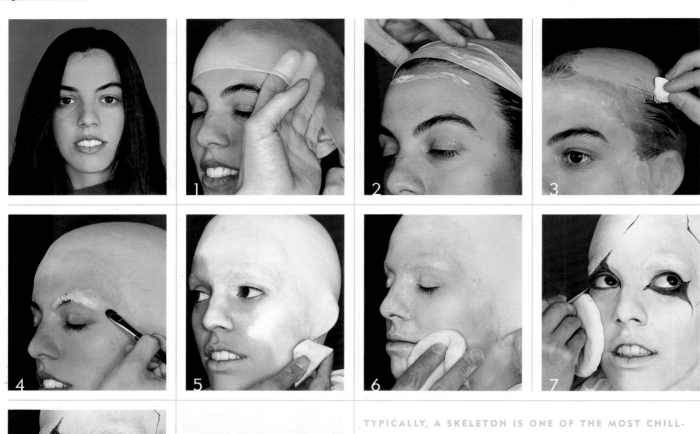

TYPICALLY, A SKELETON IS ONE OF THE MOST CHILLING HALLOWEEN FIGURES, BUT OUR MODERN VERSION HAS A SLEEK, STARTLING BEAUTY. **1.** Slick back hair, and cover head and ears with bald cap. **2.** Apply a thin line of spirit gum to skin and inside edge of cap, let dry until tacky, then press into place. Seal edges by brushing with spirit gum diluted with a few drops of alcohol. **3.** Apply flesh-toned greasepaint over cap; powder. **4.** Soften a small amount of eyebrow plastic between fingers; spread over brow in direction of hair growth. Cover with white cream makeup; blend. **5.** With sponge, cover face and head with white makeup. **6.** Powder face and cap. **7.** Using black cream makeup and eyeliner brush, line eyes, then outline crease in one eyelid, shaping upward into a triangle above the brow. On other eye, shape triangle down and to the side. Apply mascara. With a fine-tipped brush, paint cracks in skull; blacken triangles around nostrils. Use a brush and black eye shadow to shade hollows of cheeks and temples. **8.** Paint teeth outside mouth, starting in center and working outward.

mummy

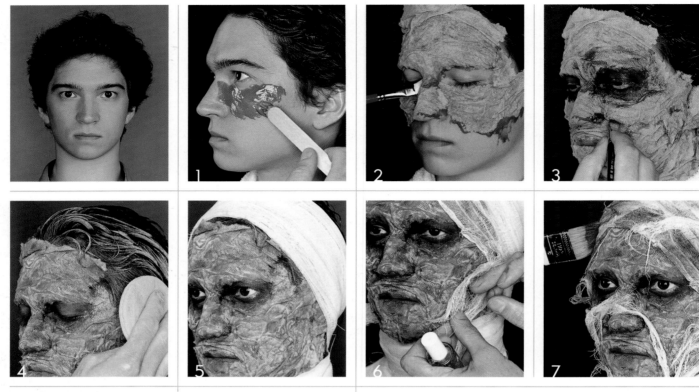

YOU WILL NEED PAPER TOWELS | COLD COFFEE | FLOUR | CORN SYRUP | BROWN AND BLACK CREAM MAKEUP | WOODEN SPATULA OR TONGUE DEPRESSOR | MAKEUP BRUSHES | NO-COLOR POWDER | CHEESECLOTH | SPIRIT GUM | PAINTBRUSH | EARTH-TONED POWDER

IT'S SIMPLE TO CREATE ANCIENT SKIN BY USING INGRE-DIENTS FROM YOUR KITCHEN. A day ahead, dip paper towels in cold coffee; without wringing, let air-dry. When ready to apply makeup, mix paste: two tablespoons flour and one tablespoon plus one teaspoon corn syrup; tint with brown cream makeup. You may need to mix more as you work. **1.** Use wooden spatula to spread paste thickly on small area of face. **2.** Tear a piece of paper towel and press over paste, tapping and wrinkling the paper. Cover entire face, including ears and eyebrows, over-lapping as necessary. Paint brown and black cream makeup around eyes, and on lips and all exposed areas. **3.** Dab makeup on bandages as well, accenting wrinkles and shading hollows of eyes and cheeks; blend. **4.** Set with powder. **5.** Wrap head and neck with cheesecloth strips. **6.** Glue loose ends to face with spirit gum. **7.** Using a paintbrush, pat bandages with brown cream makeup for an aged look. **8.** Apply earth-toned powder to lend a dusty appearance. OPTIONAL: Mix red, blue, and green food colors, then swish in your mouth. The ghastly color will last a few hours. Take care with clothes; it will stain.

WITH LAYERS OF *white feathers and turned-down yellow beak, this mask (opposite and right) suggests a snowy egret you might see wading in shallow water; more feathers splash from the wearer's upswept hair. Feathers were essential elements in the earliest costumes worn by the Celts at their annual Samhain festival, precursor to Halloween. Some societies still regard birds as bearers of celestial messages and seek to invoke their power with masks.*

bird masks

YOU WILL NEED CARDBOARD | CRAFT GLUE | COLORED ART PAPER | STAPLER | MASKS | FEATHERS

Silken feathers and paper beaks combine to make haunting bird masks. Experiment with paper to find the size and shape beak you'd like, and create a paper template for it. The basic shape is a diamond: When the beak is folded in half lengthwise, the top half should fit neatly against the mask, covering the nose. Use your template to cut out beak from cardboard. (For a hooked beak, make cuts in the cardboard and bend into a crook as desired; tape in place on the inside.) Cover beak in colored art paper, folding paper over beak and taping to the underside, or glue fabric over the beak. Staple beak to mask, then use tiny dabs of glue to add feathers, laying them along the edges of the eyeholes. The dotted feathers on the hooded-beak mask at right are guinea hen; the white feathers are turkey.

FAIRIES, IT IS SAID, *can use beauty to make humans lose their senses and become lost. If so, beware this enchanting figure (opposite and right), dressed for nightly revels. She carries a lantern, but a wand or a flute would be an equally likely accessory for one of the "little people." Her diaphanous gown and noiseless slippers counterbalance a luminous pair of organza wings and a mask and headdress adorned with silver-dollar leaves.*

fairy mask, crown, wings

YOU WILL NEED EIGHTEEN-GAUGE, WHITE CLOTH-COVERED WIRE | WHITE FLORAL TAPE | DRIED SILVER DOLLARS (MONEY PLANTS) | POLYESTER ORGANZA | WHITE RIBBON | CAT'S-EYE MASK | CRAFT GLUE

1. For the crown, measure a piece of eighteen-gauge white cloth-covered wire (available from florists and craft stores) to the circumference of child's head plus two inches. Wind white floral tape continuously around wire, adding stems of silver dollars as you go. Turn back ends in a U shape, and hook them behind head. **2.** For wings, shape floral wire into a figure 8 to size you desire; twist once at center, and secure with floral tape. Wrap each wing with a piece of polyester organza, and tie ends of the fabric in the middle of the figure 8, letting excess trail down. Add white ribbon, and let it trail down, too. For the harness: Tie a thirty-two-inch piece of ribbon at its midpoint to the center of wings. Bring ribbon halves over shoulders, then under arms; tie in back underneath wings. **3.** Replace elastic on mask with white ribbon. Glue silver dollars to mask, working from center out, overlapping them slightly.

cat and kitten

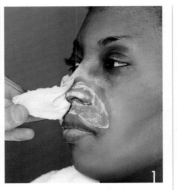

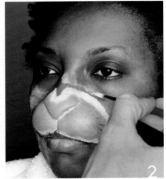

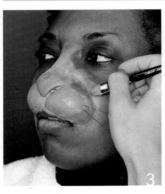

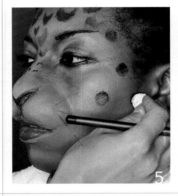

YOU WILL NEED LATEX OR FOAM CAT AND KITTEN NOSES | THICK NEEDLE | NO-COLOR POWDER | SPIRIT GUM | MAKEUP BRUSHES | ALCOHOL | FLESH-TONED GREASEPAINT | FOAM SPONGES | BLACK-BRISTLED PAINTBRUSH FOR WHISKERS | HIGHLIGHTING AND BLACK CREAM MAKEUP | EYEBROW AND EYELINER PENCIL | LIPSTICK

WITH A FELINE NOSE, A HUMAN FACE BECOMES CAT-LIKE EVEN BEFORE IT IS MADE UP. Cat noses come in latex and foam latex (foam is more realistic and flexible, but also more expensive). Don't worry if you make a mistake in positioning; alcohol softens the glue so you can remove and reapply the nose. PREPARE THE NOSE: Using a thick needle, make holes for whiskers. If necessary, cut airholes beneath nostrils. **1.** TO APPLY NOSE: Place on face, and powder, leaving an outline. Remove. Apply spirit gum to skin and inside of latex nose. Let dry until tacky, then gently press in place, using outline as a guide. **2.** Brush edges with spirit gum diluted with a few drops of alcohol to seal. **3.** To even skin tone, cover nose with flesh-toned grease-paint, blending outward with sponge. Powder. Insert whiskers (bristles from a household paintbrush). **4.** Apply highlighting cream to eyelids and brow bone. Line eyes with black cream makeup, extending liner outward on sides; blend with sponge. Fill brows with pencil, adding slight upward tilt on outside edges. **5.** Make spots with "stamp" cut out of a makeup sponge and dipped into black cream makeup. **6.** Add smaller spots with eyeliner pencil. Define creases in nose with black makeup. **7.** Use fine brush to add whisker holes. Finish with lipstick.

barroom brawler

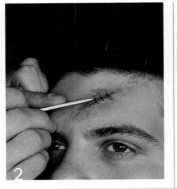

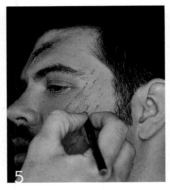

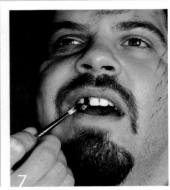

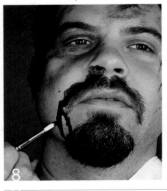

YOU WILL NEED FLESH PUTTY (SUCH AS STEIN DERMAWAX) | FLAT COTTON SWABS | FOUNDATION AND CONCEALER | NO-COLOR POWDER | WOODEN SPATULA OR TONGUE DEPRESSOR | RED BRUISE MAKEUP | FOAM SPONGES | HEAVY BLACK THREAD | SUPER GLUE | TWEEZERS OR WOODEN SKEWER | MAKEUP BRUSHES | FAKE BLOOD (SUCH AS BEN NYE FRESH SCAB) | BLACK STIPPLE SPONGE | MAROON MAKEUP | BLACK MAKEUP PENCILS | POPSICLE STICK | BLACKOUT TOOTH ENAMEL | COTTON BALL | GLYCERINE | BANDAGES

DON'T WORRY IF MAKEUP LOOKS A LITTLE SPLOTCHY; ERRATIC APPLICATION MIMICS A REAL WOUND. **1.** Use hands to soften and roll a piece of flesh putty into a ball; smooth across forehead with fingers. Smooth edges with a flat cotton swab. Blend with foundation or concealer; powder. **2.** With flat wooden spatula, make thin groove down the center of the putty, forming a gash. Use red bruise makeup to fill in; blend color around gash with sponge. For each stitch, knot two short pieces of heavy black thread together, and add a drop of super glue to hold its shape; let glue dry completely before applying to face. Use tweezers or skewer to press stitches into putty; trim threads. With makeup brush, dab fake blood in gash. **3.** Apply red bruise makeup around one or both eyes. Dab concealer high on cheekbone to make red area appear more inflamed. Powder. **4.** Use a black stipple sponge to brush maroon makeup lightly across cheek to simulate scratches. **5.** Accent scratches with a sharpened black makeup pencil. Avoid drawing a solid line; you'll achieve a more realistic effect if it's broken up. **6.** Apply thin lines of fake blood with Popsicle stick. **7.** Paint blackout tooth enamel on one or more teeth; put cotton ball under top lip for a swollen effect. **8.** Drip thick fake blood from the nose, ears, and hairline. Simulate sweat with a few drops of glycerine. Scuff knuckles as in steps 4, 5, and 6. Finish with a bloody bandage on the hand.

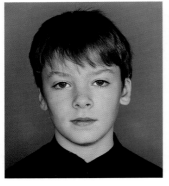

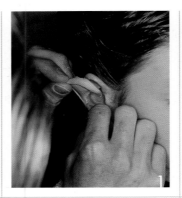

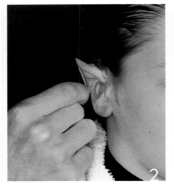

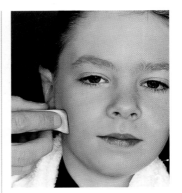

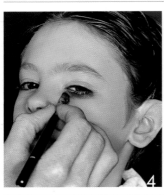

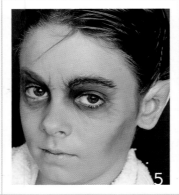

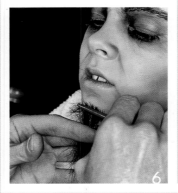

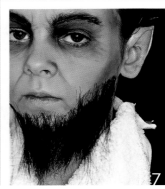

YOU WILL NEED LATEX VAMPIRE EARS | NO-COLOR POWDER | SPIRIT GUM | ALCOHOL | MAKEUP BRUSHES | GREEN, BLACK, AND WHITE CREAM MAKEUP | MAKEUP SPONGES | CASTOR OIL | COTTON SWABS | BLACK EYEBROW PENCIL | FAKE HAIR | RED HAIRSPRAY | FANGS

GREENISH SKIN AND SINISTER EYES ARE CLASSIC TRAITS OF THE UNDEAD. **1.** Fit latex vampire ears over ears; powder to create an outline. Remove. Apply spirit gum to ear and inside latex ear tip; let dry until tacky. Press in place, using outline as a guide. If you make a mistake, rub with alcohol to soften glue; remove and reapply. **2.** Seal edges by brushing with spirit gum diluted with a few drops of alcohol. **3.** Apply green makeup with sponge; add a few drops of castor oil to makeup for ears (cream makeup alone won't stick to latex). **4.** Line under eyes; blend with cotton swab. Lightly brush black cream makeup around eyes. Using eyebrow pencil, brush brows upward. **5.** Lightly shadow with gray makeup (mix white and black) in hollows of cheeks and creases around nose. Draw dark lines with brow pencil upward from inside corners of eyes and down to mouth lines. **6.** For beard, apply spirit gum to small patch of skin starting at neck. Spread a few strands of hair between fingers; press in place with brush handle. Human or yak hair is most realistic and most expensive. Crepe hair works well, but must be straightened before use. Simply unbraid it, wet it, and let it hang overnight to stretch the fibers. **7.** Layer facial hair for natural effect, working upward on neck, downward on cheeks, chin, and sideburns. Trim ends unevenly. **8.** For mustache, glue long strands over lip; trim, cutting into mustache, not across it bluntly. TO FINISH: Tease hair, spray with red hairspray; insert fangs.

V

ICTORIANS IN ENGLAND AND THE UNITED STATES WERE KNOWN TO LOVE GHOST STORIES AND TO BELIEVE IT WAS POSSIBLE TO commune with the spirit world. No less authoritative a man than Sir Arthur Conan Doyle, creator of the peerless detective Sherlock Holmes, was utterly convinced (with the help of hucksters) that spirits could be captured in photographs. Since ancient lore designated Halloween as the night when spirits easily mingled with the living, our Victorian forebears went all-out to welcome any supernatural visitors by making their houses as haunted-looking as possible. The continued broad popularity of horror stories today attests to the doggedness of their fascinations, so if you rig your house to be frightening on Halloween, it just might be possible to persuade some twenty-first-century revelers to entertain their own hazy beliefs in ghosts and goblins.

It doesn't matter if you live in an old house or a modern condominium—who's to say in this mobile era that ghosts wouldn't love to move into a new house? Whatever dwelling you have, you can make it the scariest in your neighborhood. Begin by dimming the lights and looking around. Ponder the past lives that might have filled the rooms, that might be lurking still. Then turn the lights back on and start decorating—just as your ghosts dictate.

FILMY GHOSTS *made of inexpensive polyester chiffon gossip shamelessly at the windows of Robert Kinnaman's 1785 farmhouse in Wainscott, New York, that is locally famous for its inventive annual Halloween decorations. Inside, spirits also appear in doorways, shimmer in mirrors, and hang from the rafters.*

A dramatic entrance is the first requirement of a haunted house. Like the house pictured in this chapter, a spook-friendly dwelling must be approached with a delicious mingling of excitement and fear: The door is open, the lights are on, and no one is visible except three busy specters in the first- and second-floor windows. A hundred years ago, a partygoer's arrival on the threshold might have summoned a silent, dark-robed figure extending a cold hand made from an opera glove filled with sawdust; today that would be you, ready to lead guests to an area where they can leave their coats.

The goal is to cast a spell that is mysterious and creepy, decidedly and darkly humorous. Endow the rooms with an invented history of bad luck, unsettled scores, and lovers separated by untimely death. Fill doorways, corners, windows, and mirrors with the filmy fabric spirits of your imagined housemates; bottle them in jars like genies, and let them struggle to be free. Keep furnishings spare. This evening calls for rickety straight-backed chairs—

ALL WHO DARE enter this haunted house may fish for Halloween candy bundled in gauzy fabric (how else would a ghost package treats?). A sprig of fern is tucked into the waxed twine that cinches the tops. OPPOSITE: A paper raven alights on a broken-down fence. Each slat is a crepe-paper streamer cut to a point. Vintage velvet leaves glued to the paper and strewn about the room suggest a howling wind whirling about indoors.

not upholstered cushions—and for creaky, uncarpeted wood floors. Consider removing some furniture altogether, rolling up rugs and taking down curtains. Let ectoplasm—the amorphous substance once said to be emitted by mediums during a successful seance, but usually netting dipped in luminous paint—fairly drip from the rafters. Allow the spiders to establish primacy over other inhabitants by filling the house with their webs. Construct a black crepe-paper, ramshackle picket fence, worthy of a derelict mansion, around the walls of your living room; call Poe's raven down to alight on a well-chosen stake.

Not everything has to be black and orange; an ashen palette can be equally unsettling. Lavender polyester covering a dining table in an icy cloud can be so sheer and shadowy as to seem nearly iridescent. Carve jack-o'-lanterns from blue and white and green pumpkins and squash. Banish living plants and flowers, and instead make sophisticated arrangements of dried leaves and stripped branches. Look to add subtle details specific to your own art or knickknacks: The husband and wife portraits in this chapter, painted in 1800, have chiffon masks that were whipped up for an imaginary danse macabre. Such is the stuff of which nightmares are made; just ask one of your nonbelieving guests when he wakes up on November 1.

chiffon ghosts

YOU WILL NEED POLYESTER CHIFFON | KRAFT PAPER | PUSHPINS | RUBBER CEMENT

Our ghosts and masks are made from polyester chiffon, available at fabric stores. With practice, they can be cut freehand, but you may want to try it this way first: Lay the fabric over a large sheet of kraft paper (above left) on a worktable or the floor. Sketch an outline onto the fabric with a pen or felt-tip marker, and pin the fabric to the paper. Cut out paper and cloth together—the paper makes it easier to cut the slippery fabric. There are various ways to display the ghosts. On wood, you can secure the fabric with a few discreet pushpins. On glass or mirrors, use a few dots of rubber cement; it will rub right off.

black cats

YOU WILL NEED PHOTOCOPIER | BLACK CONSTRUCTION PAPER | WHITE PENCIL | DOUBLE-SIDED TAPE | BLACK PAPER PARASOL | ACRYLIC CRAFT PAINT

To make a spitting cat, use a photocopier to enlarge the template on page 136. Trace design onto heavy black construction paper with a white pencil; cut out. Use double-sided tape to place the cats where guests might least expect to find them—here they are ready to jump out of two framed prints. To make a cat firescreen, use a black paper parasol (see the Guide), and paint its eyes with gold acrylic craft paint. Cut ears from black construction paper, poke holes in bottom, and put them over spokes of the parasol. Paint on whiskers with white acrylic craft paint. The mask over the mantel is vintage.

THE PROFILE *of a howling polyester chiffon ghost with a serpentine tongue rises up from the smoky glass of a circa-1725 scroll-top mirror. Beeswax candles glimmer on the mantelpiece amid 'Crown-of-Thorns' squash and dried bottleneck gourds. The tops of the tall, straight bottlenecks were sawed off so they could be used as vases for a few dried shoots.*

Bats in the rafters,
cats on the prowl,
Ghosts in the parlor,
the screeching of an owl;
When a house is haunted,
you must believe,
Or 'tho doors are open,
none may ever leave.

THESE NINETEENTH-CENTURY *portraits are usually hung facing one another; for a Halloween masquerade party, they look the other way so they won't reveal their identities. The strings of their chiffon masks are tucked behind the frames to keep them in place without harming the paintings.* OPPOSITE: *Construction-paper bats of different sizes play with perspective—one appears frighteningly close; two keep a safer distance.*

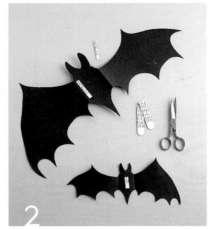

bat silhouettes

YOU WILL NEED PHOTOCOPIER | KRAFT PAPER | BLACK
CONSTRUCTION PAPER | DOUBLE-SIDED TAPE

1. Photocopy and enlarge template on page 135 to
a variety of sizes. Our bats range from six inches to
three feet across. For large sizes, trace template in
sections on kraft paper, then tape together (or draw
freehand). Trace template onto black construction
paper using white pencil; cut out. Cut bat out in sections and tape together, as with template, if necessary.
2. Make folds at sides of bat to suggest flapping
wings. Use double-sided tape to attach bats to the wall.

A COOL RECEPTION *befits
visitors to a haunted house,
so don't make yours too
cozy; keep furnishings spare.*
RIGHT: *This dining-room
table is draped in a cloud
of ashen lavender chiffon
that billows across the floor.
The arrangements on the
mantlepiece were made with
pale dried Cecropia leaves;
fabric spirits sing from the
mirror over the fireplace.*
OPPOSITE: *Small chiffon
ghosts hover in glass jars, im-
prisoned with dots of rubber
cement. An open-topped com-
pote holds an appropriately
named 'Little Boo' pumpkin
and a white eggplant.*

A MENACING *silhouette of a prowler, whose ominous long shadow climbs the stairs, produces the kind of thrill a trick-or-treater craves on Halloween. Since the height of risers doesn't vary much from staircase to staircase, these papers can be put away and used again next year, perhaps to haunt another house.*

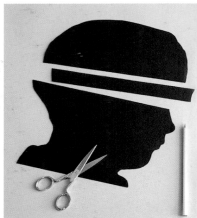

staircase silhouette

YOU WILL NEED KRAFT PAPER | BLACK PAPER | DOUBLE-SIDED TAPE

To make a silhouette for your staircase, tape a long sheet of kraft paper to the wall of a dark room. Have someone hold a menacing or dignified pose in front of a single light source so that the shadow falls completely on the paper in a size appropriate to your staircase. Trace the outline. Count the number of stair steps, and measure the height of the risers and the nosing (the protruding front edge of the step between the risers). With a pencil and ruler, divide shadow shape into sections corresponding to risers and nosers. Cut out, discarding strips that correspond to the nosing and numbering the others on the back as you go. Use these pieces to cut identical shapes from black paper; number those pieces, too. Attach to the risers with double-sided tape.

scary sound effects

SOMETIMES, HALLOWEEN JUST HAPPENS TO LAND ON A BEAUTIFUL DAY. CURSES! Don't let a little sunshine spoil your fun; you can brew your own storm at home and make it as clamorous as you like. This chart offers a few examples of how ordinary household items can be used to fill your house with mischievous poltergeists. Once you've mastered a few sound effects, use them to create a soundtrack for scary story-telling (enlist the help of a partner who can work behind the scenes), or tape-record your repertoire and turn up the volume when trick-or-treaters come knocking. Unleash a thunderous gale every time you open the door, or supplement with the Bach D Minor fugue or your best werewolf howl, and you may even scare up some real ghosts.

fire

Crinkle a piece of cellophane or waxed paper to mimic a crackling flame. For large fires, use several sheets and several pairs of hands.

ghostly footsteps

Slowly knock the heels of leather-soled shoes together or against a wooden floor to achieve the sound of footsteps coming from the attic.

wind

Fold a sheet of waxed paper over a comb. Hum or blow softly with your lips against the paper-covered teeth for a howling wind.

thunder

Grasp one side of a sheet of poster board. Shake hard to make a thunderclap; taper off for distant, echoing rumbles.

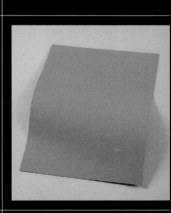

rain

Pour dry, uncooked rice into a metal tray or baking pan. Vary the speed for realistic-sounding rain; accompany with thunder as you wish.

gurgling bog

Use a drinking straw to blow bubbles at the surface of a bowl of water. Vary the rhythm of the bubbles to bring the slimy bog eerily to life.

yum

PUMPKIN-CARVING FEAST | GHOULISH SUPPER | *CRAFTY PARTY* | WICKEDLY GOOD MENUS

aT THIS PARTY, THE GUESTS AREN'T
WEARING THEIR BEST CLOTHES,
AND THEY AREN'T MINDING THEIR MANNERS. THEY'RE
dressed for warmth and work, reaching and grabbing across the
table, brandishing utensils, and talking all at once. Such raucous
behavior is welcome on this occasion. This is not a formal dinner,
after all. It's a pumpkin-carving feast.

The whole time-honored business of carving Halloween pumpkins
becomes even more festive and messy when pursued in the company
of friends and family. A party like this is best held outdoors, although
all that's really needed is a work surface, aprons, and carving tools—all
readily available to city dwellers without yards. But it's hard to imagine
a better setting than this eighteenth-century farm in Chester County,
Pennsylvania. Under a bright-blue October sky, the rolling grounds
are strewn with the fire-red leaves shed by black walnut trees.

Nature provides the essentials for such a gathering, but there is
plenty for a host or hostess to do. A sturdy, old table was taken outside and covered with kraft paper to serve as the pumpkin-carving
station. Each place was set with a carving board and a canvas apron
with carving tools rolled up inside. Hardware and art-supply stores
stock the carving tools—miniature saws, carving knives, linoleum
cutters, hole cutters, and wood gouges. Raid your kitchen drawers

*IT'S A TREAT to attend an
outdoor party in the fall,
as long as you're dressed for
it; guests attending this
pumpkin-carving feast at
a Pennsylvania farm have
blankets and thermoses
full of Hot Spiced Concord-
Grape Juice to keep warm.
Pumpkin-carving candidates
line up along the steps to
the house and on a sturdy
table by the door. When the
carving is done, a buffet
lunch will be served outside.*

SEE "WICKEDLY GOOD
MENUS" FOR RECIPES

for the melon baller and cookie cutters. Scrapers and fleshing tools are ideal for cleaning out pumpkins. (For instructions on how to use a variety of such tools, see "Lighting the Night" and "Conjuring a Glow.") Provide buckets for scooped-out seeds, and baskets for the parsnips, carrots, pea pods, radishes, and peppers that will become idiosyncratic noses, ears, and eyes when poked into a pumpkin shell. Wool blankets will be welcome on a cold day; also give guests their own thermoses of heated Concord-grape juice and bowls of toasted pumpkin seeds to munch on as they carve.

Of course, you will need a lot of pumpkins. More than one hundred million are grown in the United States each year, the majority of them to be hollowed out, carved, and set on doorsteps and windowsills in late October. Be sure to choose some of the many pumpkins that come in colors other than orange. Include some pale, moon-shaped 'Lumina' and 'Flat White Boer' pumpkins

PARTY FARE designed for young and old includes white bean and turkey sausage stew served in sugar pumpkin bowls; accompany it with pumpkin-seed biscuits and a salad of string beans, endive, honey-baked pecans, and tart dried cranberries. You might offer figs, pears, and apples beside a cheeseboard; this one features a generous wedge of farmhouse cheddar. The table looks as bountiful as a farm stand, rich with the fruits of the harvest.

among the candidates. There are red and green and blue varieties, too. The best carving pumpkins, regardless of color, are heavy for their size, with a nice curly stem.

Even guests who have not carved a pumpkin in a decade or more are sure to dive back into the task with unabashed delight. When the carving is done, serve a leisurely lunch on a rustic outdoor table piled high with imaginative seasonal fare—try a menu featuring savory leaf-shaped hand pies, stew served in hollowed-out pumpkin bowls, a great pumpkin cake, and caramel apples. Guests can sit on wooden chairs and eat comfortably from plates balanced in their laps. Later, as the sky darkens, ceremoniously hand out candles and illuminate the fresh lanterns. The guests will smile, and Jack will smile back.

menu

TOASTED PUMPKIN-SEED BISCUITS | PUMPKIN BUTTER | CINNAMON-CLOVE APPLE BUTTER | WHITE BEAN AND SAUSAGE STEW IN PUMPKIN SHELLS | MAPLE-WALNUT OATMEAL COOKIES | CRUNCHY GREEN BEAN SALAD | SAVORY AUTUMN LEAF PIES | FARMHOUSE CHEDDAR WITH FIGS, PEARS, AND APPLES | CARAMEL APPLES | HOT SPICED CONCORD-GRAPE JUICE | THE GREAT PUMPKIN CAKE

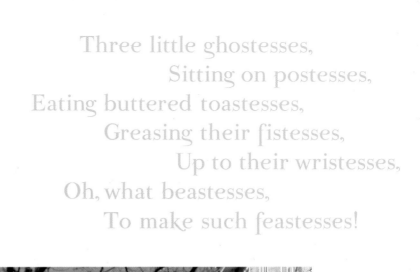

Three little ghostesses,
        Sitting on postesses,
Eating buttered toastesses,
        Greasing their fistesses,
                Up to their wristesses,
Oh, what beastesses,
        To make such feastesses!

EXAMPLES OF *a minimal-ist approach to pumpkin carving boast slitty triangle eyes and root-vegetable noses (opposite).* THIS PAGE, CLOCKWISE FROM TOP: *Three generations work together at the carving station. Guests impart personalities to their pumpkins. A work-in-progress displays a variety of carving techniques. A wheelbarrow holds fat lantern candidates. Each carving kit includes tools in a canvas apron wrapped around a dishtowel; children's kits have plastic utensils (adults will help with the tougher carving).*

vegetable jack-o'-lanterns

YOU WILL NEED HOLE CUTTER | MINIATURE SAW | CHILE PEPPERS | RADISHES | PEA PODS | PARSNIPS

Use a hole cutter and a miniature saw to make a horned pumpkin (below left). Cut a hole in the back of the pumpkin, and hollow out the inside. Use saw to cut a high, wide mouth with room for chile-pepper teeth, which are attached to the shell with straight pins. Use a hole cutter to make holes for the eyes and horns. Stuff eye sockets with radishes (position radishes so their roots make brows; carve into the centers for irises); green chiles make curved horns. Choose your own simple cuts to give faces to 'Lumina' pumpkins (below right), and attach vegetable noses, ears, and eyebrows with straight pins.

A MOTLEY PARADE *of finished orange and white jack-o'-lanterns lines up along a wooden bench (opposite). Horns, hair, eyebrows, and facial features made with parsnips, carrots, pea pods, and chile peppers imbue each one with a distinct personality.* ABOVE: *Ten-year-old triplets show off their chosen pumpkins.*

LUNCH IS SERVED

(clockwise from top left): A grinning host and hostess descend the stairs with trays of hollowed sugar pumpkins filled with White Bean and Sausage Stew. The leafy pies have two fillings: roasted carrots, parsnips, garlic, and Swiss chard; and cider-glazed shallots with Granny Smith apples; a mug of Hot Spiced Concord-Grape Juice accompanies the meal. The cookies are rich with oats, maple syrup, walnuts, and coconut. String bean and endive salad is served in a generous old wooden bowl.

CELEBRATING *the harvest (clockwise from near right): Crunchy Green Bean Salad and Toasted Pumpkin-Seed Biscuits make tasty sides for the stew. Savory Autumn Leaf Pies were shaped with a leaf cookie cutter (a toothpick was used to draw veins in the leaves). Three friends perch atop giant pumpkins to eat from miniature ones. The buffet table includes homemade apple and pumpkin butters, figs, pears, apples, farmhouse cheddar, breadsticks, and a loaf of pumpernickel bread.*

HOMEMADE CARAMEL APPLES, *plain or dipped in nuts, appeal to children and make a nostalgic treat for adults. Decorative leaves and stick handles were gathered from the lawn and rinsed before use.* OPPOSITE: *For dessert, a buttermilk pumpkin cake made in two Bundt pans is joined together with melted chocolate, coated with an orange butter glaze, and dressed with chocolate leaves. The stem is a twisted paper bag covered with floral tape.*

LTHOUGH KIDS THRILL IN AN-
TICIPATION DURING THE WEEKS
LEADING UP TO HALLOWEEN, THE TIME CAN BE TRYING
for their parents. Some years, the level of children's indecision about
their costumes is exceeded only by their anxiety over design and
production. When the costume and the holiday finally come, the
parents get their share of enjoyment, trailing their little ones from
house to house, savoring the spectacle toward which everything
has been building, and pinching candy from junior's treat bag.
But then it's all over, and as children gather to indulge in their
annual, one-night-only candy-eating marathon, parents often
find themselves sentenced—let it be said, unjustly—to pizza jail.

Prisoners, free yourselves! Halloween night commands most
of the elements of a first-rate party: good company, fancily or
fancifully dressed; a charged atmosphere full of laughter and shadows; candlelight; and a rare stretch of free time, particularly for a
school night. The only missing ingredient is real food with a solid
measure of adult silliness dedicated to its presentation—in other
words, a menu that combines good tastes with bad jokes.

Let everyone know to make your house the last stop on their
trick-or-treat rounds. Those who have been keeping close watch
over the children will particularly appreciate being greeted with

LURE A GAGGLE OF
weary adults to your table
without spending too
much time slaving over a
hot cauldron—you must
fly, after all. Set a buffet
with an irresistible assort-
ment of bewitching, nutri-
tious treats: The Devil's
Salsa served with Tortilla
Spikes, Mauled Apple
Cider, cheesy Croaked
Messieurs, and Ancient
Eggs to be rolled in salt
and black sesame seeds.

SEE "WICKEDLY GOOD
MENUS" FOR RECIPES

A FROZEN DRINK IS
*tempting enough, but a
Piña Ghoulada (below left)
served in a "blood"-rimmed
martini glass is irresistible.
Corn syrup stained with
food coloring enhances the
drink's devilish sweetness.*
OPPOSITE: *A martini packs
more than the usual punch
when garnished with ice-
cube eyeballs; it's the very
definition of an adult treat.
For the younger set, use
the frozen eyeballs to chill
flavored seltzer.*

an Eyeball Highball—a martini served up with all-seeing radish-and-olive ice cubes. Or perhaps they will prefer a Piña Ghoulada, a rum libation poured into a martini glass whose rim drips with corn-syrup blood. The red food coloring has the extra dividend of imparting a ghoulish look to the drinker's lips. Anyone expected to drive the broomstick home will find comfort at the end of a ladle dipped in a burbling cauldron of Mauled Apple Cider, which has been laced with cinnamon, cloves, and star anise. Place a tray of deliciously gruesome Ladies' Fingers on the bar—knobby witch-digit pretzels sporting halved-almond fingernails.

Pile high the platters for the buffet. You might dress up like an undead waitress to serve wicked "sandwitches" that you have advertised in a spidery hand on a black-board: the B.A.T. (bacon, arugula, and tomato); G.H.O.S.T. (goat cheese, herbs, oak-leaf lettuce, sun-dried tomatoes, and tapenade); All Hallow's Cheese (with Branston

PIÑA GHOULADAS

pickle on pumpernickel); and the late, lamented Croaked Monsieur, gooey with melted cheese and ham. An appetizer of savory garlic soup will keep vampires at bay so mortal guests may sup undisturbed. Tortilla Spikes (brushed with oil and chili powder before baking) invite stabs at The Devil's Salsa. A Decomposed Salad of roasted butternut squash, shallots, endive, and pumpkin seeds appeals to any parent's by-now ravenous hunger for noncandy comestibles. And remember, adults don't reject sugar on this night, they just don't want a dessert torn from paper wrappers in frantic succession. Give them sundaes topped with licorice-and-chocolate spiderwebs.

Most buffet preparations can take place among the other tasks set aside for Halloween day. Deliciously poisonous-looking Ancient Eggs must be made three days ahead. Final assembly of the sandwitches, soup, salsa, and salad is easily accomplished in the evening before the revelers return from their rounds of trick-or-treating. Whichever soul stays home to hand out candy can handle this aspect of the preparations. Grateful guests will praise you for giving them something both malicious and nutritious to sink their fangs into, and it's even possible that a few kids will wade through the ocean of M&M's to see what all the groaning (with pleasure) is about.

VAMPIRES won't appreciate this garlic soup with black-cat pumpernickel toasts, but mortal guests need not fear their neighbors' scorn: After fifteen minutes of simmering, garlic loses its bite. The sinfully rich stock is thickened with potatoes and smoothed with Marsala wine. Invite guests to garnish each bowlful with freshly grated Parmesan and chopped chives.

SHOO VAMPIRE SOUP

G.H.O.S.T. SANDWITCH

THE DEVIL'S SALSA

PUT GUESTS *under a grateful spell with holiday fare including (clockwise from top left) a G.H.O.S.T. Sandwitch (goat cheese, herbs, oak-leaf lettuce, sun-dried tomatoes, and tapenade); The Devil's Salsa served with Tortilla Spikes; Croaked Messieurs—the ultimate ham-and-cheese combo; and All Hallow's Cheese, pumpernickel topped with melted cheddar and a dollop of Branston pickle.*

CROAKED MESSIEURS

ALL HALLOW'S CHEESE

MAULED APPLE CIDER *can be wicked (spiked with rum or whiskey) or just plain good, kept simmering with sticks of cinnamon, star anise, and lady apples stuck with cloves.* OPPOSITE: *In the spirit of this night of transformations, Ancient Eggs are hard-cooked, then steeped in a brew of strong tea and soy sauce for three days. The peeled eggs, looking like cool marble, are meant to be rolled in coarse sea salt and toasted black sesame seeds.*

MAULED APPLE CIDER

LADIES' FINGERS

NO SELF-RESPECTING *witch would be caught dead eating a plain scoop of vanilla ice cream, but a spiderweb spun across a sundae (right) suggests a decidedly dastardly gourmand.* OPPOSITE: *Never mind what kind of ladies these fingers come from. They make lovely—or at least tasty—appetizers for a Halloween gathering.*

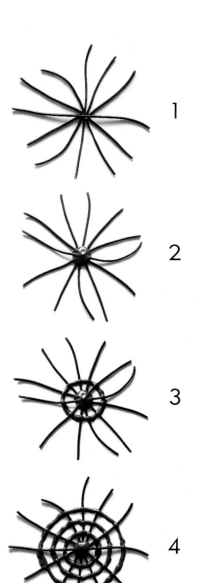

1

2

3

4

SPIDERWEB SUNDAE

spiderweb sundae

YOU WILL NEED WAXED OR PARCHMENT PAPER | NINE STRANDS OF THIRTY-EIGHT-INCH BLACK LACE LICORICE | SIX OUNCES SEMISWEET CHOCOLATE CHIPS, MELTED AND SLIGHTLY COOLED | PASTRY BAG WITH #3 PLAIN TIP | VANILLA ICE CREAM

FOR EACH WEB: **1.** On a piece of waxed or parchment paper, make an X with two five-inch pieces of licorice; fill in with eight shorter pieces to make a loose asterisk. **2.** Pour melted chocolate into the pastry bag, and pipe a large chocolate dot in the center of the web, uniting the licorice strands. **3.** Pipe a circle about a half inch from the center, over each piece of licorice. **4.** Draw two or three more concentric chocolate circles, moving away from center. Let stand one hour; peel off paper, and garnish your ice cream. The webs can be stored in a cool place for up to two days. Makes eight sundaes.

[*CRAFTY PARTY*]

SAY SOMEONE YOU CONSIDER CREATIVE ASKS YOU IF YOU ARE "CRAFTY": SHE ALMOST CERTAINLY IS NOT QUESTIONING YOUR HONESTY. IT'S more likely she perceives you to be a kindred spirit, one of the people who like to make things with their hands. If you count yourself among that number, you're a good candidate to throw a crafty party, for which all the decorations are handmade. Bring out the crayons and tempera to make a homemade invitation, of course; include a request that all the costumes be original, in keeping with the theme. Plan the party around a few craft projects for your guests to work on together—grown-ups as well as children. The result will be a Halloween party as rich in possibility as the night itself.

Like the crafty Victorians who established the full-fledged holiday we celebrate today, you have a ball decorating virtually every surface in the house—doors, stairs, walls, windows, tabletops. Most of the projects in this chapter are made with paper, perhaps the material most closely associated with invention. Cut, folded, colored, stamped, painted, or shredded, paper can make Halloween decorations as scary and alluring as a witch's gingerbread house. The drama and simplicity of a black-and-orange or black-and-white color scheme allows you to play with almost any arrangement of strong graphic elements and still conjure just the right atmosphere.

A RARE *autumn butterfly comes calling, drawn like a moth to the flickering pumpkins and paper luminarias banking the doorway of this frame house. Plump and decidedly oversized spiders and insects climb the walls, but the effect is enthralling, even to a youngster normally not fond of bugs. Her antennae have picked up the intended signal: Tricks are welcome and treats await revelers who dare to knock.*

A TREAT TABLE *is layered with four paper tablecloths, cut to size, trimmed decoratively, and block stamped with images of ramshackle fences and flying bats (templates on page 135). Candy overflows from painted metal buckets and stuffs cellophane bags cinched with licorice whips. Black-and-orange paper-plate masks on paint stirrers (facial features were cut from adhesive labels) await guests beneath a "shredded" curtain of black crepe-paper streamers.*

Some of the projects here are more complicated than others and should be done several days before the party, including the crepe-paper costumes, "torn" curtains, and the spiderweb tablecloth. Tasks that are kid-friendly and can be enjoyed with the party under way include small cakes stenciled with colored sugar and paper-plate masks mounted on wooden paint stirrers; block-stamped treat bags and home-packaged surprise bundles can be stuffed with enough candy to give kids an enviable jump start on trick-or-treating.

You may be surprised at our unbridled enthusiasm for crepe paper, a material that has lost standing in recent years, mainly used in the production of two-color garlands for prom night. But the United States was once smitten with the stuff. Jodi Levine, deputy crafts editor at MARTHA STEWART LIVING, has amassed an impressive collection of crepe-paper craft books, most from the fifties, full of ingenious home and holiday decorating and sewing projects. Jodi found crepe paper almost magical from a crafts point of view: It can be stretched, twisted, ruffled, curled, braided, sewn, and even worn—what medium could be more suitable for Halloween's contortions and distortions?

For the costumes in this chapter, folds of crepe paper were cut and sewn into butterfly wings, bewitching bonnets of sunflowers, and caps of upended roses and lilies of the valley. Flitting around in a butterfly trance or grinning beneath crowns of petals, children assume the role of woodland fairy with ease, and it's an appropriate one for this night: Paying respect to fairies was an important element of the Samhain ritual. The Celts believed it was best to stay in their good graces; legend said that they would steal your children if you didn't feed them and keep a clean house but give you gifts and money and help out with chores if you did. Flowers are as essential to fairies as to us, and are said to be worn as hats and gloves by those who dance at night throughout the emerald woodlands. The spirit conjured by these paper-flower caps and filmy wings is one of pure playfulness, surely the most important dimension of the good-natured mischief encouraged on Halloween.

If you want to be you, and yet not you,
Dress in a costume old or new,
Many others I plan to ask
So wear a wig or at least a mask,
Come at 7 o'clock and don't be late,
The rest of the time we'll leave to fate!

spooky invitations

YOU WILL NEED COMPUTER POSTCARD PAPER | MASKING TAPE | ORANGE AND FLUORESCENT CRAYONS | FOAM BRUSH | BLACK TEMPERA PAINT | ETCHING TOOLS: TOOTH-PICKS, NAILS, PLASTIC UTENSILS, COFFEE STIRRERS

These fluorescent invitations can be made even by young children, if supervised. Print party information—time, date, place, address—on one side of computer postcard paper (eight-and-a-half-by-eleven-inch sheets perforated into four sections). Use masking tape to secure paper text side down to a work surface. Evenly tape the entire border of each card. Color cards completely with bright-orange and fluorescent crayons, then use a foam brush to coat entire surface with a thick layer of black tempera paint. Once the paint has dried, ask your favorite young artist to etch designs into the black paint, revealing glowing color beneath. Vary your etching tools; the kitchen drawer is a good place to find suitable implements. Frame extra cards against orange construction paper, and use as wall decorations on party night.

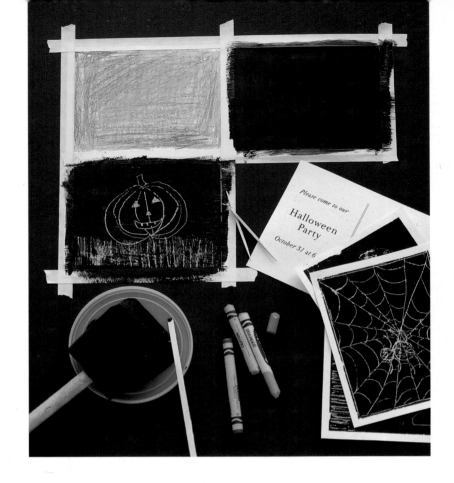

block stamping

YOU WILL NEED PHOTOCOPIER | FOAM PLATES | UTILITY KNIFE | SPRAY ADHESIVE | FOAM BOARD OR CARD-BOARD | SMALL FOAM-EDGE ROLLER | ACRYLIC PAINT

Photocopy your choice of templates (see pages 135–37), enlarging them as necessary. **1.** With a pen, etch designs onto the flat center of a foam plate; cut out shape with a utility knife. Use spray adhesive to attach each shape to a square of foam board or corrugated cardboard. **2.** With a small foam-edge roller, coat each raised shape with acrylic paint, using another foam plate as a roller tray. Press the "inked" stamp onto paper or fabric. If you want to layer images, let the paint dry a bit before adding the second image. For the goody bags on page 112, use plain-paper envelopes in black and white. Seal them, then snip off one edge with decorative shears to make an opening. Stamp with acrylic paint in the opposite color.

treat table

YOU WILL NEED CARDBOARD | DOUBLE-SIDED TAPE |
BLACK CREPE PAPER | DECORATIVE SHEARS OR ROTARY
CUTTER | PHOTOCOPIER | ORANGE PAPER PLATES | GLUE
STICK | ORANGE GLASSINE | WOODEN PAINT STIRRERS |
ACRYLIC PAINT | CRAFT GLUE | TWELVE-INCH BLACK
PAPER PLATES | UTILITY KNIFE | SELF-ADHESIVE LABELS

1. For torn curtains (page 107), first make a "curtain rod" of two cardboard strips, as wide as your window frame. Lay one strip on work surface, and apply double-sided tape. Attach crepe strips all across. Repeat for four layers. Loosely fold all paper up from the bottom, to a point just below the support. Cut vertically through all thicknesses with decorative shears or rotary cutter, creating long strips; unfold paper. Add one more layer of tape, then second strip of cardboard. Cover second strip with crepe paper. Tack above window; snip bottoms for a ragged edge. **2.** For pumpkin masks, transfer enlarged template (see page 136) onto orange paper plate, and then use it to cut paper plate into proper shape. Coat front of plate with glue stick, then add a sheet of orange glassine. Add another layer of glue, avoiding holes; repeat until you have four layers of glassine. Trim excess around edge of mask. Paint a paint stirrer as a handle. Glue to back of plate, at bottom. **3.** Make cat masks from twelve-inch black paper plates. Transfer enlarged template (see page 136) to plate; cut out. Cut long strips from another plate for whiskers; glue to back. Cut eyeholes with utility knife. For facial features, transfer from templates, and cut shapes from self-adhesive labels; peel, and stick onto plate.

A GIRL PROPERLY *attired in an orange party dress peers through a paper-plate mask depicting a surprised black cat. Using features prepared in advance, such masks are fun for young revelers to assemble and sport on Halloween.*

A SUNFLOWER *and a lily of the valley bask in unusual circumstances—the light of a full moon, which is actually a giant collapsible paper globe painted with a dashing silhouette of a witch on the wing. Another young guest hides himself behind a black paper-plate mask he made; pom-pom spiders*

witch lantern

YOU WILL NEED ROUND, WHITE PAPER LANTERN | PHOTOCOPIER | SOFT LEAD PENCIL | PAINTBRUSHES | BLACK ACRYLIC PAINT

Cast a plain, round, white paper lantern in the light of the moon by having a witch sweep across it in fine style. This is not a difficult project, but you may want to recruit a friend to steady the collapsible paper orb while you work. You may also find it helpful to place one hand inside the lantern to support the surface as you work on it. Photocopy and enlarge template on page 136, and cut it out. Hold it against the lantern, and use a soft lead pencil to trace around it very gently so as not to puncture the paper. With a fine-tipped brush dipped in black acrylic paint, go over the outline; start filling in the narrowest parts; switch to a wider brush for the interior of the shape if you wish. Hang to dry, then hang over a decorated table. After the holiday, it can be folded flat and stored for next year.

spider's table

YOU WILL NEED ROUND BLACK TABLECLOTH | TAILOR'S CHALK | RIBBON | IRON-ON ADHESIVE | POM-POMS | PAINTBRUSH | CRAFT GLUE | SATIN RATTAIL CORD

1. Position black tablecloth on table. Use a ruler and tailor's chalk to lay out each strand of the web—eight spokes and as many rings as will fit on tabletop. Position outermost ring just inside the edge of the table. For the spokes, you'll need four ribbons longer than the tablecloth's diameter, and sets of eight ribbons in graduated lengths for each ring. Using iron-on adhesive, iron ring pieces in place along chalk markings. Add spokes so that they all cross in the center and hide the "seams" where the ring pieces meet. **2.** Add pom-pom spiders. For each spider, you need two small pom-poms in slightly different sizes. Brush on a little glue to join them together; let dry. For the legs, cut four six-inch lengths of satin rattail cord in same color as pom-poms; tie knots about a quarter of the way in from each end to make joints in the legs. Glue the four cords parallel to one another across one side of the larger pom-pom (the spider's belly). Tie small knots of cord for eyes and glue on top of small pom-pom (the head), clipping ends close. **3.** Safety pin spiders to ends of ribbons on tablecloth.

PLAIN BLACK cotton block stamped with jack-o'-lanterns that blaze with three expressions—happy, mean, and scared—can be sewn up into a charming dress or boy's vest. Or just embellish store-bought clothing. Stamps were coated with fluorescent-orange paint, which shows up best. OPPOSITE: Greeting-card envelopes make graphic goody bags when sealed and snipped open on one side and block stamped with single and layered holiday images in opposite colors.

USE STENCILS *to decorate party cakes (opposite) with sanding-sugar silhouettes of the emblems of the holiday. Turn cakes over before decorating; the smooth, even cake bottoms make the best surface for stenciling.* LEFT: *Our glossy black-and-orange paper cup and plate combo can be accomplished with the sole aid of decorative shears or patterned rotary cutter. The trimmed plate or cup is paired with the same item in a contrasting color.*

party plates and cups

YOU WILL NEED PAPER PLATES AND CUPS IN CONTRASTING COLORS | DECORATIVE SHEARS OR PATTERNED ROTARY CUTTER

Color and line are the keys to this dramatic paper-plate combination. Use pinking or other decorative shears, or a patterned rotary cutter to trim the edge of a paper plate. Lay that plate on top of a second plate of the same size in a contrasting color. To cut a decorative edge around a cup, a rotary cutter is the most effective tool. Rest the cup on the edge of a cutting surface placed on a table so that the lip of the cup can hang just over the edge of both. This way the paper won't crimp as you work your way around the cup's rim, cutting from the inside. Slide the opposite-color cup inside the trimmed cup.

stenciled cakes

YOU WILL NEED PHOTOCOPIER | STIFF PAPER | UTILITY KNIFE | BROWNIES AND GINGERBREAD | COOKIE CUTTERS | ORANGE AND WHITE SANDING SUGAR

Photocopy stencils onto stiff paper using the templates on pages 135 and 136. Cut out with utility knife. Cut cooled brownies and gingerbread cakes into circles and squares. Position stencil, and sift sanding sugar (or a mix of ground ginger and confectioners' sugar) generously over cake. Carefully lift stencil. See "Wickedly Good Menus" for detailed instructions.

A TRAY OF *tightly packed crepe-paper pumpkins looks ready for the oven, but actually they're ready to be torn open and spill their treats. Each pouch has been stuffed with sweets and small toys and closed with a stem made by wrapping green floral tape around the twisted-closed paper. We gave curly ends to the foliage by winding the floral tape tightly around a pencil.*

A PEGBOARD *spray-painted orange and laid flat on a table makes an ideal serving tray for these gussied-up round-headed lollipops. Dressed like symbols of the holiday—pumpkins, spiders, and ghosts—each is made with two circles of same-size crepe paper tied above or below the candy and closed with string or floral tape.*

crepe-paper party favors

YOU WILL NEED ORANGE, BLACK, AND WHITE CREPE PAPER | LOLLIPOPS |
GREEN FLORAL TAPE | NINE-INCH BLACK PIPE CLEANERS | STRING | CANDY

1. For pumpkin lollipop, cut two circles of orange crepe paper three-and-a-half inches in diameter. Stack them; poke lollipop through center of circle. Pull papers up to neck of round candy, and twist over the top. To make stem, trim excess paper and seal pumpkin with green floral tape, making the foliage curly by wrapping tape tightly around a pen and sliding pen out. For spider, use same measurements to cut two sheets of black paper. Align, and place lollipop in center, pulling paper down around it to neck. Seal with transparent tape. Twist a nine-inch black pipe cleaner once around base to make two legs. Repeat twice. Bend legs an inch from body and turn up ends to make feet. For ghost, cut two circles six inches across from white crepe paper. Align, and place lollipop in center, pulling paper down to neck. Tie loose paper with string at neck. **2.** For pumpkin pouches, cut two ten-inch circles from orange crepe paper. Stack circles; place goodies in center. Gather paper just above treats; twist a little to close. Secure with green floral tape wrapped around base of twist, binding upward to make stem. Add foliage as with lollipop, if desired.

BENEATH THE *crepe-paper petals of her rose cap, a young girl extracts candy from a paper pumpkin made from an orange gift bag twisted at the top and wrapped with green seam binding for a convincing stem. Available at craft stores, colored paper bags— imaginatively trimmed with scissors and decorative hole punches—make cheerful conveyances for creepy gummy worms and wax fangs.*

1

2

3

treat bags

YOU WILL NEED ORANGE AND BLACK PAPER BAGS | BLACK AND ORANGE PAPER | HOLE PUNCH | SHOELACE | ONE-HALF-INCH CRAFT PUNCH | PINKING SHEARS | GREEN SEAM BINDING

You can create enticing packages for party candy with colored paper bags. If the bags aren't flat-bottomed, fold the corners under to make them stand after you've added the candy. **1.** Use scissors to cut the top of an orange bag into a row of points. Cut black paper to fit inside as a sleeve, and zigzag cut its top, too. Insert sleeve in bag, and fold both over together. Punch two small holes near the top through all layers; thread a black shoelace through from the back, and tie a bow. **2.** Trim the top of a black bag straight, then use a one-half-inch craft punch to make big round holes. Line bag with a sleeve of orange paper; zigzag top with pinking shears. **3.** Trim one inch from the top, then gather top together and secure it with rubber band. Hide rubber band with green seam binding to suggest a stem. Wind binding from bottom to top and back down again; tie it off in a little knot at back.

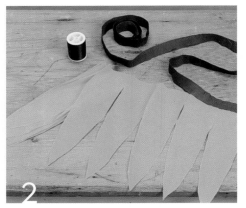

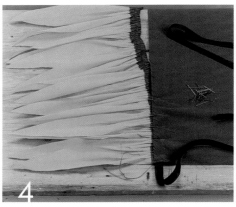

A COSTUME doesn't have to make you into another person; you can be a blossom instead. Here children glow as a sunflower (below) and a rose (below opposite), faces framed in exuberant petals sprouting from their green leotard "stems." Crepe paper is sized tissue, and behaves more like fabric than paper—as long as you don't tug too hard.

sunflower bonnet

YOU WILL NEED TAPE MEASURE | BROWN AND YELLOW CREPE PAPER | SEWING MACHINE | RIBBON

Measure head from earlobe to earlobe, and add two inches for bonnet piece. **1.** Cut brown crepe paper to this length and to height of the sheet (twenty inches); fold in half lengthwise. Set aside. For petals, cut yellow crepe paper twice as long as the bonnet piece and ten inches wide. Accordion fold and trim one end as shown; unfold. **2.** Make "bias tape" from strip of brown crepe four inches wide and as long as unfolded strip of petals; fold long edges of tape to center, then fold in half. Pin straight edge of petal strip to bias strip; machine sew with a loose stitch, leaving long thread ends. **3.** Pull threads to gather petals and bias tape to width of reserved bonnet piece. **4.** Pin bias tape between open edges of bonnet piece; sandwich in a piece of ribbon for a tie at each end. Stitch. **5.** Loosely stitch opposite edge of bonnet, and pull threads to gather. Knot threads to secure.

rose or lily-of-the-valley cap

YOU WILL NEED TAPE MEASURE | GREEN, COLORED, AND WHITE CREPE PAPER | SEWING MACHINE | FLORAL TAPE | CRAFT GLUE | GREEN THREAD-COVERED WIRE

Start with a green cap. Measure around head, adding one and a half inches. Cut crepe paper to that length and double the height you wish cap to be. Height of cap follows paper's grain. **1.** Fold crepe in half lengthwise; folded edge will be cap bottom. Machine-stitch ends of paper together. With hands, twist top, and bind with floral tape. **2.** For rose cap, cut individual crepe-paper petals in teardrop shape with one squared-off end. We used five four-and-a-half-by-nine-inch petals (length runs with grain) for a ten-inch-high cap. Overlap slightly, join with loose stitch; gather tightly. Place atop cap, cinch petals and stem together; secure with floral tape. For jagged green sepals, cut a nine-inch-tall strip as wide as circumference of cap. Fold into pleats one and a half inches wide; cut one end of folded paper into a deep V. Unfold; cut Vs into spikes. Wrap around cap stem, cinch, and fix with floral tape. Cut out leaves. Dab backs with a tiny line of craft glue; lay a length of green thread-covered wire on leaf to attach. Use floral tape to join leaves to stem. Stretch centers of petals to curl them. **3.** The lily-of-the-valley (see page 110) also begins with a green cap. Cut white crepe paper to same width as cap and ten inches high. Fold in accordion-pleats as wide as petals will be. Trim one end as shown. Sew ends together; cinch top. Set petals on cap, and cinch both "stems" together. Bind with floral tape. **4.** Cut out leaves with short stems; crease each in half lengthwise (with the grain), stretching paper on both sides. Join leaf and cap stems with floral tape. Stretch centers of petals to make them curve upward.

A MONARCH *butterfly (opposite) needs only a black leotard and antennae to accompany her black-and-yellow crepe-paper-and-wire wings.* ABOVE: *Tiny gathers give crepe paper a wonderful stretchiness that lets it hold shapes, as in the petals of this pink rose hat.*

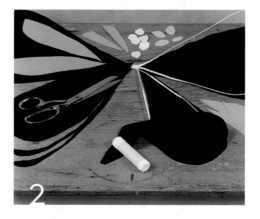

butterfly costume

YOU WILL NEED WHITE THREAD-COVERED WIRE | WHITE FLORAL TAPE | BLACK AND COLORED CREPE PAPER | GLUE STICK | BLACK VELVET RIBBON | VELCRO DOTS | PLASTIC HEADBAND

To make the base for the wings, we used white thread-covered wire, but other kinds of wire can be used. Since ours came in precut lengths, we joined lengths with white floral tape when a longer piece was needed. **1.** Shape the wire into four loops for the wings; the ends of each loop of wire should join at the point that will be the center of the wings. Floral-tape joints of each loop together, creating a short "stem" of wire. Tape four stems together at center. **2.** For each wing section, cut two pieces of black crepe paper about one-quarter inch larger than wire form. Run glue stick around the edge of one piece; carefully place wired frame on top of glued area. Repeat with the other paper piece for that section and position, sandwiching wire between. Repeat process for other three sections. Trim away excess paper from the edges. Cut out shapes in contrasting colors to decorate the wings; attach them with dabs from a glue stick. To make straps for the wings, stitch the end of a length of black velvet ribbon around the center of the wings, hiding any visible white tape; repeat with a second ribbon. To hold the wings in place, run ribbons over the wearer's shoulders and around to her back; mark the spot where they intersect in the center of her back. Attach Velcro dots to the ribbons at that point. Trim excess ribbon. To make the antennae, twist the center of a twenty-inch length of wire several times around the middle of a plain plastic headband, leaving the wire ends pointing up. Wrap each wire with a narrow strip of black paper to proper length, and twist to tighten. Add ends of antennae: Loosely roll up two two-by-eight-inch strips of crepe paper, add a dab of glue, and slip it over antennae; twist to tighten at the bottom. Snip a little with scissors to feather ends. Wrap another strip of paper around headband, gluing it at the beginning and end.

pumpkin-carving feast

WHITE BEAN AND SAUSAGE STEW IN PUMPKIN SHELLS
SERVES 12

Pearl onions are easier to peel after being soaked for five minutes in very hot water. You can prepare the beans the night before you make the stew: Place them in a medium bowl, cover with two inches of cold water, and soak overnight.

   2 cups dried navy beans
  12 small sugar pumpkins, about 2 pounds each
      (see the Guide)
  ¼ cup olive oil
      Coarse salt and freshly ground pepper
   2 dried bay leaves
   2 sprigs of fresh thyme, plus leaves for garnish (optional)
   1 teaspoon whole black peppercorns
   5 cups Homemade Chicken Stock (recipe follows)
      or low-sodium canned chicken broth
   1 large onion, roughly chopped
   3 tablespoons unsalted butter
   2 large leeks, trimmed and thinly sliced crosswise,
      well washed
   4 medium carrots, cut into ¼-inch rounds
   1 celery stalk, strings removed, diced
  36 red or white pearl onions, peeled
  12 ounces small red fingerling or new potatoes,
      halved lengthwise
   1 pound turkey sausage, cut into ½-inch pieces
   1 cup baby peas, fresh or frozen, defrosted
   8 ounces white-button mushrooms, wiped clean, quartered
  ¼ cup all-purpose flour
  1¼ cups milk
   2 tablespoons fresh sage, coarsely chopped

1. If you prepared the beans the night before, start with step 2. Place the beans in a large saucepan, cover with cold water by 2 inches, and bring to a strong boil over high heat. Cover, and remove from the heat; let stand for 1 hour.
2. Preheat oven to 350°F. Cut a lid into the top of each pumpkin. Remove the seeds and pulp, and reserve the seeds for toasting. Rub the inside of each pumpkin with olive oil, and sprinkle lightly with salt and pepper. Place the pumpkins, right side up, and lids on parchment-lined baking sheets, and bake for 30 minutes. Turn the pumpkins over, and continue to bake until tender but firm, about 30 minutes more. Set aside.
3. Place the bay leaves, thyme, and peppercorns in a 6-inch square of cheesecloth. Draw up the edges, and tie the bundle with a piece of kitchen twine; set aside. Drain navy beans, and place in a medium stockpot. Add the chicken stock, onion, and cheesecloth bundle. Cover, and bring to a boil; reduce heat, and simmer, still covered, until the beans are tender, about 30 minutes. Drain the beans, reserving the cooking liquid. Discard the cheesecloth bundle.
4. In a large stockpot, melt the butter over medium-high heat. Add the leeks, carrots, celery, pearl onions, and potatoes. Cook until softened, about 12 minutes. Add the sausage, and cook until browned, about 5 minutes. Stir in peas and mushrooms. Sprinkle in flour, and cook 2 minutes. Reduce heat to medium, add the milk and reserved cooking liquid, and stir the stew until it thickens, about 20 minutes. Stir in reserved beans and sage. Divide stew among the pumpkins, and return to oven; bake until pumpkins are soft and stew is heated through, about 15 minutes. Garnish with thyme leaves, if using, and place reserved lids on top. Serve hot.

HOMEMADE CHICKEN STOCK
MAKES 5 QUARTS

When using stock for a specific recipe, begin making it at least twelve hours ahead of time, and refrigerate for eight hours so the fat has a chance to collect on top and can be removed.

   2 leeks, white and pale-green parts,
      cut into thirds, well washed
   1 teaspoon whole black peppercorns
   6 sprigs fresh dill or 2 teaspoons dried
   6 sprigs fresh flat-leaf parsley
   2 dried bay leaves
   2 carrots, cut into thirds
   2 celery stalks, cut into thirds
   1 four-pound chicken, cut into 6 pieces
  1½ pounds chicken wings
  1½ pounds chicken backs
   2 forty-eight-ounce cans (3 quarts) low-sodium
      chicken broth, skimmed of fat
   6 cups cold water, or more

1. Place leeks, peppercorns, dill, parsley, bay leaves, carrots, celery, whole chicken, wings, and backs in a large stockpot. Add chicken broth and water, cover, and bring to a boil. Reduce to a very gentle simmer, and cook, uncovered, about 45 minutes. The liquid should just bubble up to the surface. A skin will form on the surface; skim it off with a slotted spoon, and discard, repeating as needed. After about 45 minutes, remove the whole chicken from the pot, and set it aside until it is cool enough to handle.

2. Remove the meat from the chicken bones, set meat aside, and return bones to the pot. Transfer meat to the refrigerator for another use; if you plan to use it in soup, shred meat before refrigerating it.

3. Continue to simmer stock mixture, on the lowest heat possible, for 3 hours, skimming foam from the top as needed. The chicken bones will begin to disintegrate. Add water if at any time the surface level drops below the bones.

4. Fill a large bowl with ice and water; set aside. Strain the stock through a fine sieve or a cheesecloth-lined strainer into a very large bowl. Discard solids. Transfer bowl to ice bath; let stock cool to room temperature.

5. Transfer stock to airtight containers. Stock may be labeled at this point and refrigerated for 3 days or frozen for up to 4 months. If freezing, leave the layer of fat intact; it seals the stock. If refrigerating, chill for at least 8 hours and remove fat before using.

CRUNCHY GREEN BEAN SALAD
SERVES 12

½ cup honey
  Pinch of cayenne pepper
1½ cups pecans
  3 tablespoons sherry vinegar
  2 teaspoons Dijon mustard
  ¾ teaspoon coarse salt
  ½ cup walnut oil (see the Guide)
  2 pounds string beans, trimmed
  ¾ cup dried cranberries (see the Guide)
  2 heads Belgian endive, trimmed and sliced lengthwise
  Freshly ground black pepper

1. Preheat oven to 350°F. Place honey and cayenne in a small saucepan; heat until warm. Stir in pecans. Line a baking pan with a Silpat baking mat (see the Guide) or parchment paper. Pour mixture onto prepared pan. Bake until dark golden brown, about 25 minutes. Set aside to cool.

2. In a small bowl, whisk together the vinegar, mustard, and salt. Slowly drizzle in the walnut oil, whisking constantly, until mixture is emulsified. Set aside.

3. Fill a large bowl with ice and water; set aside. Bring a medium stockpot of water to a boil. Add string beans; cook just until tender, about 2 minutes. Drain; immerse in ice bath. Remove, pat dry, and place in a large bowl. Toss with dressing. Add nut mixture, dried cranberries, and endive. Add pepper to taste; toss gently. Serve immediately.

TOASTED PUMPKIN-SEED BISCUITS
MAKES 1 DOZEN

  2 tablespoons shelled pumpkin seeds
  2 cups all-purpose flour, plus more for work surface
  1 teaspoon coarse salt
  1 tablespoon plus 1 teaspoon baking powder
  ½ teaspoon cream of tartar
  1 tablespoon sugar
  8 tablespoons (1 stick) unsalted butter, chilled and cut into pieces
  ⅔ cup plus 1 tablespoon nonfat buttermilk
  1 large egg white, lightly beaten

1. In a small skillet over medium-high heat, toast the pumpkin seeds, shaking pan frequently until they are golden brown and beginning to pop, about 6 minutes. Set aside.

2. Preheat oven to 400°F. Line an 11-by-17-inch rimmed baking sheet with parchment paper, and set aside.

3. In a large bowl, combine flour, salt, baking powder, cream of tartar, and sugar. Using your fingers or a pastry cutter, cut butter into flour mixture. Combine until mixture resembles coarse meal. Carefully mix in buttermilk just until it is incorporated. The mixture should appear crumbly.

4. Turn out the dough onto a lightly floured, clean work surface. Lightly press the dough together to form a ³/4-inch-thick disk. Using a 2-inch round biscuit cutter, cut out 12 biscuits, and transfer to the prepared baking sheet. Using a pastry brush, lightly coat the tops of each biscuit with egg white, and sprinkle with toasted pumpkin seeds. Bake until golden brown, about 12 minutes. Serve warm.

PUMPKIN BUTTER
MAKES 2 CUPS

Sugar or pie pumpkins will yield the best texture for this recipe.

  1 two-pound sugar pumpkin, seeded, peeled, and cut into 2-inch chunks (see the Guide)
  ½ cup packed dark-brown sugar
  ¾ teaspoon ground cinnamon
  ¼ teaspoon ground nutmeg
  1 teaspoon freshly grated ginger
  2 tablespoons freshly squeezed lemon juice, strained

1. Preheat oven to 350°F. Place pumpkin pieces in a roasting pan, and cover tightly with aluminum foil. Bake until pumpkin pieces are very tender, about 45 minutes. Transfer to the bowl of a food processor, and process until smooth.

2. Transfer the puréed pumpkin to a medium saucepan, and cook over medium-low heat, stirring often, until very thick, about 25 minutes. Stir in the brown sugar, cinnamon,

nutmeg, ginger, and lemon juice; cook until sugar is dissolved, about 5 minutes. Cool and serve, or store in the refrigerator, in an airtight container, up to 1 week.

SAVORY AUTUMN LEAF PIES
MAKES 1 DOZEN

The dough and fillings for these small pies can be made a day ahead of time and stored in the refrigerator until ready to use. If you want to make only one of the fillings, double that recipe.

3¾ cups all-purpose flour, plus more for board
¾ teaspoon coarse salt
1 tablespoon sugar
¼ cup plus 2 tablespoons pure vegetable shortening
12 tablespoons (1½ sticks) cold unsalted butter, cut into pieces
½ cup plus 2 tablespoons ice water
1 large egg yolk
3 tablespoons heavy cream

FOR HARVEST VEGETABLE FILLING:

1 carrot, diced in ½-inch pieces
1 parsnip, diced in ½-inch pieces
½ head garlic (½ ounce)
1 tablespoon olive oil
1 teaspoon coarse salt
¼ teaspoon freshly ground pepper
1 tablespoon unsalted butter
½ small yellow onion, finely chopped
4 ounces Swiss or red chard (leaves and stems), washed and chopped

FOR APPLE-SHALLOT FILLING:

1 tablespoon unsalted butter
5 medium shallots, thinly sliced lengthwise
2 tablespoons sugar
½ cup apple cider
½ Granny Smith apple, peeled and diced into ¼-inch pieces
¼ teaspoon coarse salt
1 teaspoon fresh thyme leaves

1. In the bowl of a food processor, combine the flour, salt, and sugar. Add the shortening and butter; pulse until mixture resembles coarse meal, about 30 seconds. Pulse in ice water just until mixture comes together. Divide the dough in half. Transfer each half to a piece of plastic wrap; flatten into disks. Wrap tightly; refrigerate for at least 1 hour, or overnight.

2. To make harvest vegetable filling, preheat oven to 425°F. Place carrots, parsnips, and garlic in a small roasting or baking pan. Drizzle with olive oil, and toss until coated. Season with ½ teaspoon salt and the pepper. Roast in oven until golden and tender, about 30 minutes. Transfer carrot mixture to a bowl. Squeeze out garlic from cloves, and add to carrots and parsnips; combine. Set aside.

WHITE BEAN *and sausage stew is proffered in tureens of hollowed-out sugar pumpkins; the wooden serving platter is dressed with pumpkin vines.*

3. Reduce oven temperature to 375°F. Heat butter in a medium skillet over medium-high heat. Add onion, and cook until translucent, about 1 minute. Add chard; season with remaining ½ teaspoon salt. Cook until soft, about 4 minutes. Drain; toss with carrot mixture. Set aside to cool.

4. To make apple-shallot filling, heat butter in a medium skillet over medium-high heat. Add shallots and 1 tablespoon sugar; cook until soft, about 3 minutes. Add remaining tablespoon sugar; stir until shallots begin to brown, about 4 minutes. Raise heat to high, add ¼ cup cider, and cook until all cider has been absorbed, about 2 minutes. Stir in remaining ¼ cup cider and diced apples, and lower heat to a simmer until absorbed, about 5 minutes. Stir in salt and thyme; remove from heat, and set aside to cool.

5. Line two 11-by-17-inch baking sheets with parchment paper; set aside. In a small bowl, whisk together the egg yolk and the heavy cream, and set aside. On a clean, lightly floured board, roll out half of the dough to ⅛ inch thick. Using a 4-inch leaf-shaped cookie cutter, cut out 12 leaves from the dough. Place on baking sheet. Put a heaping tablespoon of harvest vegetable filling on 6 leaves and a heaping tablespoon of apple-shallot filling on the remaining 6 leaves. Roll out remaining dough. Cut out 12 more leaves; using a toothpick, etch veins on the leaves. Brush the edges of each filled leaf with the egg mixture, and top with a veined leaf. Carefully press the edges together to seal the pies. Brush each pie with egg glaze, and place in the refrigerator to chill, about 30 minutes.

6. Remove pies from the refrigerator, and bake in the oven until golden brown, about 30 minutes. Serve warm.

A SAVORY FILLING *is sandwiched between autumn leaves of buttery pie crust. Each leaf is etched with "veins" using a toothpick.*

CINNAMON-CLOVE APPLE BUTTER
MAKES 2 ²/₃ CUPS

    2 pounds firm apples, cut into quarters
    ½ cup apple cider
    ½ cup water
  1½ cups packed dark-brown sugar
    2 teaspoons ground cinnamon
    1 teaspoon ground cloves
    ½ teaspoon ground allspice
      Grated zest and juice of 1 lemon

1. Place apples, cider, and water in a large saucepan over medium-high heat. Cover, and bring to a boil; reduce heat, and simmer until apples are soft, about 20 minutes. Remove from heat. Pass mixture through a food mill fitted with a medium disk, and return to the saucepan.
2. Stir in brown sugar, cinnamon, cloves, allspice, lemon zest, and lemon juice. Place saucepan over low heat, and cook, stirring occasionally, until very thick and dark brown, 2½ to 3 hours. Watch mixture carefully as it thickens so as not to scorch. Cool completely, and serve, or store, refrigerated, in an airtight container, up to 2 weeks.

HOT SPICED CONCORD-GRAPE JUICE
MAKES 1 GALLON

If fresh Concord-grape juice is not available from your local farmers' market, the supermarket variety will work fine.

    1 gallon Concord-grape juice
    8 cardamom pods
    4 sticks cinnamon
    1 teaspoon freshly ground nutmeg

In a medium stockpot, combine Concord-grape juice, cardamom, cinnamon, and nutmeg. Cover, and bring the mixture to a boil; reduce heat. Simmer until the juice becomes infused with the spices, about 20 minutes. Serve immediately, or keep warm until ready to serve.

THE GREAT PUMPKIN CAKE
SERVES 16

You will need two eight-inch Bundt pans. To make a stem, twist a brown-paper lunch bag into a stem shape, and wrap it tightly with green floral tape (see the Guide). Insert the stem into the center of the cake. Remove before serving.

    1 tablespoon unsalted butter, plus more for pans
    ¾ cup Dutch-process cocoa powder, sifted, plus more for pans
    2 cups sugar
    2 cups all-purpose flour
    2 teaspoons baking soda
    1 teaspoon baking powder
    ½ teaspoon coarse salt
    2 large eggs
    2 teaspoons pure vanilla extract
    ½ cup canola oil
    ¾ cup nonfat buttermilk
    ¾ cup milk
    3 ounces hazelnut or milk chocolate
    3 ounces bittersweet chocolate
    7 ounces heavy cream
      Orange Butter Glaze (recipe follows)
      Chocolate Leaves (recipe follows)

1. Preheat oven to 350°F. Generously butter the inside of two 8-inch Bundt pans; dust lightly with cocoa powder.
2. In the bowl of an electric mixer fitted with the paddle attachment, combine sugar, flour, cocoa, baking soda, baking powder, and salt; set aside.
3. In a medium bowl, whisk together the eggs, vanilla, canola oil, buttermilk, and milk. Slowly add the egg mixture to the sugar mixture. Mix the batter on low speed until smooth, about 1 minute. Divide batter evenly between the prepared pans. Bake cakes until a cake tester inserted into the center comes out clean, about 40 minutes. Transfer to a cooling rack, and cool for 20 minutes before removing from the pans.
4. Place both chocolates, heavy cream, and remaining tablespoon butter in a medium heat-proof bowl, or the top of a double boiler, over a pan of gently simmering water. Heat, stirring often, until chocolate is completely melted, about 5 minutes. Remove from heat, and let cool to room temperature. Whisk chocolate until lightened; set aside.
5. Using a serrated knife, trim the bottoms of both cakes so they are both flat. Spread the chocolate evenly on the flat side of one of the cakes. Invert the remaining cake onto the chocolate so that a pumpkin shape is formed. Transfer the cake to a wire rack.

6. Working quickly, carefully pour the orange butter glaze over the cake, tilting the cake as necessary to coat all sides of the cake. Let the glaze set completely before garnishing with chocolate leaves. Serve.

ORANGE BUTTER GLAZE
MAKES 2 CUPS

    5 tablespoons milk
      A few drops of orange liquid-paste food coloring
      (see the Guide)
    4 cups sifted confectioners' sugar
    1 cup (2 sticks) unsalted butter, melted

In a small bowl, combine the milk and the orange food coloring until the mixture reaches desired color, and set aside. In a medium bowl, whisk together the sugar and the melted butter. Add the milk mixture, and continue whisking until smooth. Use immediately.

CHOCOLATE LEAVES
MAKES ABOUT 20

Use leaves that have not been sprayed with any chemicals. Leaves can be made up to one day ahead of time.

    20 ivy, black walnut, or rose leaves, about 2½ inches long
      4 ounces hazelnut or milk chocolate, chopped

1. Wash the leaves, and dry thoroughly. Set aside on a rimmed baking sheet lined with parchment paper. Place chocolate in a medium heat-proof bowl, or the top of a double boiler, over a pan of gently simmering water. Stir occasionally until the chocolate is melted. Remove from heat.

2. Using a soft ¼-inch pastry brush, coat the underside of each leaf with a thin layer of chocolate. Place the leaves in the refrigerator until firm, about 15 minutes.

3. Brush the leaves with a second layer of chocolate, and chill again. When firm, carefully peel the leaf from the chocolate. Set chocolate leaves on baking sheet, and store in the refrigerator until ready to use. Use within a day.

CARAMEL APPLES
MAKES 6

If the caramel becomes too stiff to coat the apples, rewarm it slightly over medium heat until it softens. In place of store-bought dowels, you can gather twigs that are about six inches long to use for the handles.

    2 cups nuts, such as almonds or hazelnuts (optional)
    6 small Granny Smith or other firm apples (about 1½ pounds)
    1 cup sugar
    ¼ cup dark corn syrup
    1 cup heavy cream
    2 tablespoons unsalted butter

1. If using nuts, preheat oven to 350°F. Spread the nuts on a rimmed baking sheet. Toast until fragrant, about 6 minutes. Transfer the nuts to a bowl to cool. If using hazelnuts, rub them while warm in a clean kitchen towel to remove skins. Roughly chop the nuts, and set aside.

2. Carefully wash and dry twigs, if using. Insert a 6-inch twig or wooden dowel into the center of each apple. Transfer apples to an 11-by-17-inch rimmed baking sheet lined with a Silpat baking mat (see the Guide) or parchment paper. Set aside. Fill a large bowl with ice and water; set aside.

3. Place sugar, corn syrup, heavy cream, and butter in a small saucepan; bring mixture to a boil over medium-high heat, stirring to combine. Clip on a candy thermometer, and boil the mixture until the temperature reaches 250°F (the hard-ball stage), about 20 minutes. Immediately plunge the saucepan into the ice bath to stop the cooking. Working quickly, dip apples one at a time into the caramel, and place them on the lined baking sheet. Roll the bottom of the apples in the toasted nuts, if using. Transfer to a serving platter as soon as set, and serve immediately.

MAPLE-WALNUT OATMEAL COOKIES
MAKES 1 DOZEN

    1½ cups old-fashioned oatmeal
     ¾ cup desiccated (unsweetened) coconut
    1⅓ cups all-purpose flour
     ½ teaspoon coarse salt
     ⅔ cup packed light-brown sugar
      8 tablespoons (1 stick) plus 1 tablespoon unsalted butter
      3 tablespoons pure maple syrup
      2 tablespoons golden syrup (see the Guide)
      1 teaspoon baking soda
      2 tablespoons boiling water
      1 teaspoon pure maple extract
      1 cup (2¾ ounces) walnuts, coarsely chopped

1. Preheat oven to 300°F. Line two 11-by-17-inch baking sheets with parchment paper, and set aside. In a medium bowl, combine oatmeal, coconut, flour, salt, and brown sugar. Set aside.

2. In a small saucepan over medium heat, combine butter, maple syrup, and golden syrup. Heat until butter is melted. Remove from heat, and set aside. In a small bowl, combine baking soda with boiling water. Immediately stir this mixture into the melted butter until combined. Add the maple extract; stir into the oat mixture. Fold in the walnuts.

3. Form dough into 2¼-ounce balls, about 3 tablespoons each, and place onto prepared cookie sheets about 3 inches apart, six to a sheet. Flatten each of the balls slightly.

4. Bake cookies until golden brown and set, about 20 minutes. Transfer to a wire rack to cool. Store in an airtight container, up to 1 week.

ghoulish supper

SHOO VAMPIRE SOUP
SERVES 8 TO 10

- 5 heads garlic
- 2 tablespoons unsalted butter
- 4 leeks, white and pale green parts only, thinly sliced, well washed
- 8 sprigs fresh thyme
- 8 sprigs fresh flat-leaf parsley
- 1 tablespoon whole black peppercorns
- 1 dried bay leaf
- 2 pounds Yukon gold potatoes, peeled and cut into 1-inch dice
- 4 fourteen-and-a-half-ounce cans low-sodium chicken broth, or 7 cups Homemade Chicken Stock (page 125)
- ¼ cup Marsala wine
- 1 cup heavy cream
- 2 teaspoons coarse salt
- 1 teaspoon freshly ground black pepper
- ½ teaspoon freshly grated nutmeg
- 8 to 10 slices pumpernickel bread
- ¾ cup freshly grated Parmesan cheese
  Snipped chives, for garnish

1. Preheat oven to 450°F. Wrap 3 heads of garlic in aluminum foil; roast for 45 minutes. Let cool, halve crosswise, and squeeze garlic from cloves. Reserve garlic purée, discarding papery skins. Peel remaining 2 heads garlic.

2. In a 6-quart stockpot, melt butter over medium-low heat. Add leeks and garlic cloves; stirring frequently, cook until translucent but not browned, 20 to 25 minutes. Wrap thyme, parsley, peppercorns, and bay leaf in a piece of cheesecloth; tie with kitchen twine. Add to pot along with potatoes, stock, and garlic purée. Raise heat to medium; simmer until potatoes are tender, 25 to 30 minutes. Discard cheesecloth bundle. Pass soup through a food mill fitted with a fine disk. Discard solids; return soup to pot. Add wine; simmer over medium-low heat, about 15 minutes. Stir in cream; season with salt, pepper, and nutmeg.

3. Cut bread with cat-shaped cookie cutter. Place on baking sheet; toast in oven, 3 to 4 minutes. Serve soup in bowls; garnish with Parmesan, chives, and black-cat toasts.

EYEBALL HIGHBALLS
SERVES 4

Look for small radishes, so they will fit in your ice-cube tray.

- 14 small radishes
- 7 pimiento-stuffed olives, halved crosswise
- 16 ounces gin or vodka
- 1 ounce vermouth

1. Trim stem and root ends of each radish. Use a paring knife to scrape red skin from radish, leaving just enough to give a veiny appearance. With a small melon baller, cut a hole in the radish, about ½ inch in diameter. Fit an olive half, cut side facing out, into the hole. Place radish in ice-cube tray. Repeat with remaining radishes. Fill tray with water; freeze.

2. Mix gin or vodka with vermouth; stir with ice. Divide eyeball ice cubes among four chilled glasses. Strain martini; pour into glasses, and serve.

PIÑA GHOULADAS
SERVES 10 TO 12

This mixture can be made several hours in advance and chilled. The food coloring might give your lips a vampirish look.

FOR THE "BLOOD":

- 3 tablespoons light corn syrup
- ¼ teaspoon red food coloring

FOR THE GHOULADA MIXTURE:

- 20 ounces pineapple juice, or more to taste
- 1 fifteen-ounce can cream of coconut
- ½ cup heavy cream
- 1 cup freshly squeezed orange juice
- 10 ounces good-quality rum (optional)

1. Pour the corn syrup in a shallow bowl. Dip a toothpick into the food coloring, and stir a very small amount into the syrup to combine. Holding a martini glass by the stem, dip rim into the syrup mixture, and turn glass, coating entire rim. Turn the glass upright, allowing mixture to drip down sides. Dip the remaining glasses. Set aside.

2. Whisk together the pineapple juice, cream of coconut, heavy cream, orange juice, and rum, if using. Place 2½ cups ice in the jar of a blender, and add 1 cup of the drink mixture. Blend until smooth; add more pineapple juice if mixture is too thick. Repeat with more ice and another cup mixture until all mixture is used. Carefully pour into prepared glasses; serve.

G.H.O.S.T. SANDWITCHES
MAKES 8

Five ingredients that begin with letters spelling "ghost" gave this sandwich its name.

- 2 logs goat cheese
- ⅓ cup chopped fresh herbs, such as parsley, basil, or marjoram
- 8 sandwich rolls, such as ciabatta or pan bagnat
  Tapenade (recipe follows)
- 1 ten-ounce head oak-leaf lettuce
- 1½ cups sun-dried tomatoes soaked in olive oil
  Olive oil for drizzling
  Coarse salt and freshly ground pepper

1. Roll goat cheese in chopped herbs; slice into ¼-inch-thick rounds. Cut rolls in half; spread with tapenade.

2. Layer rolls with lettuce, goat cheese, and sun-dried tomatoes. Drizzle with olive oil, and sprinkle with salt and pepper. Top with remaining bread, and serve.

TAPENADE
MAKES 1⅓ CUPS

2 cups pitted kalamata olives
¾ cup fresh flat-leaf parsley leaves

Pulse olives and parsley in the bowl of a food processor until coarsely chopped. Tapenade will keep refrigerated, in an airtight container, up to 4 days.

TORTILLA SPIKES
SERVES 8

You will need to make these in two batches.

¼ cup olive oil
1 teaspoon chili powder
12 flour tortillas
1½ teaspoons coarse salt

1. Preheat oven to 350°F. Combine the oil and chili powder in a small bowl. Brush each tortilla with the oil mixture, and sprinkle with salt.
2. Cut into 1-inch-wide strips, and arrange in a single layer on two baking sheets. Bake until crisp and golden brown, 8 to 10 minutes.

THE DEVIL'S SALSA
MAKES ABOUT 5 CUPS

The spiciness will vary, depending on the heat of your peppers. Add a little at a time, until it's as spicy as you like.

2 ears fresh corn, kernels shaved from the cob
3 tablespoons olive oil
1 orange bell pepper
1 fifteen-and-a-half-ounce can black beans, rinsed and drained
1 mango, peeled, pitted, and cut into ¼-inch dice
1 hot red pepper, seeds and ribs removed, finely diced, or more to taste
½ red onion, finely diced
Juice of 2 limes (about 5 tablespoons)
1 teaspoon coarse salt

1. Preheat oven to 450°F. Place corn on a baking sheet brushed with 1 teaspoon olive oil; roast until kernels begin to brown, about 10 minutes. Set kernels aside to cool.
2. Place pepper on gas burner; roast until charred on all sides. Transfer to bowl; cover with plastic wrap. When cool, peel off charred skin with your fingers, and remove stem and seeds. Chop into ¼-inch dice; place in large bowl.
3. Add corn, beans, half the diced mango, hot red pepper, onion, lime juice, remaining oil, and salt; toss to combine.
4. Finely chop remaining mango until a thick purée forms; stir into salsa.

FRENCH SALADE COMPOSÉE *is acknowledged in our Decomposed Salad: butternut squash and mixed greens, dotted with roasted pumpkin seeds.*

ALL HALLOW'S CHEESE
MAKES 8

4 slices pumpernickel bread
8 ounces cheddar cheese
½ cup Branston pickle (see the Guide)

Halve bread slices diagonally. Heat the broiler with a rack in the top third of oven. Slice cheese, ¼ inch thick; cut diagonally. Top each bread slice with a triangle of cheese; place on a baking sheet. Broil until cheese melts and begins to brown, 3 to 4 minutes. Transfer to a platter; top with spoonfuls of Branston pickle. Serve.

ANCIENT EGGS
MAKES 1 DOZEN

To crack eggshells without damaging eggs, roll them gently with the palm of your hand on a countertop until the entire shell is finely cracked.

1 dozen large eggs
2 quarts strong black tea, such as Earl Grey
¼ cup soy sauce
1 tablespoon coarse sea salt
3 tablespoons black sesame seeds

1. Fill a large bowl with ice and water; set aside. Place eggs in a 6-quart saucepan, and cover with cold water by 2 inches. Bring to a boil over high heat, and cook 1 minute. Remove from heat, cover, and let stand for 10 minutes. Drain, and transfer to the ice bath.

A HUNGRY GHOUL *in the* Last Chance Diner *would be well-advised to order the B.A.T. Arugula makes the difference in this twist on the BLT.*

2. Crack the eggs, leaving the shell on, and place in a large glass bowl. Cover with tea and soy sauce; refrigerate, covered, for 3 days. Remove shells. Combine salt and sesame seeds, and serve with eggs.

CROAKED MESSIEURS

MAKES 1 DOZEN SMALL SANDWICHES

- 3 tablespoons unsalted butter, *room temperature*
- 1 loaf French baguette, *sliced ½ inch thick on the bias (24 slices)*
- ¼ cup Dijon mustard
- 12 ounces Black Forest ham, *thinly sliced (12 to 14 slices)*
- 12 ounces Gruyère cheese *(grated on large holes of box grater to yield ¾ cup)*

1. Spread 2 tablespoons butter on one side of each slice of bread, and mustard on the other. Fold ham to fit on bread. Layer cheese, ham, and more cheese on mustard side of one bread slice; top with second bread slice, mustard side down.
2. Melt a third of the remaining butter in a sauté pan over medium heat. Place four sandwiches in the pan; cook, using a lid smaller than the pan to press down sandwiches. When they are golden brown, flip sandwiches, and cook on other side until golden brown. Repeat with remaining butter and sandwiches, wiping out pan with a paper towel between batches. If not serving immediately, sandwiches may be reheated in a 350°F oven for about 5 minutes.

MAULED APPLE CIDER

SERVES 12

- 20 whole cloves
- 5 lady apples
- 1 gallon apple cider
- 2 cinnamon sticks
  Zest of 1 orange, *removed in large strips with a vegetable peeler*
- 6 star anise

Press 4 cloves into each lady apple. Place cider, cinnamon, orange zest, and studded lady apples in a large pot, and warm over medium-low heat. Let steep 1½ hours, without boiling, until aromatic and flavorful. Garnish with star anise.

DECOMPOSED SALAD

SERVES 8

- 1 butternut squash, *peeled, seeded, and cut into ¾-inch cubes*
- ¼ cup olive oil
- 2 teaspoons coarse salt
  Freshly ground black pepper
- 2 shallots, *peeled and sliced ¼ inch thick*
- 2 tablespoons sugar
- ¾ teaspoon ground cinnamon
  Pinch of cayenne pepper
- ½ cup pumpkin seeds
- 1 teaspoon honey
- 2 tablespoons balsamic vinegar
- 1 six-ounce head red or white endive, *leaves separated*
- 1 ten-ounce head red-leaf lettuce, *torn into bite-size pieces*

1. Preheat oven to 450°F, and position a rack in the lower third of the oven. Combine butternut squash, 1 tablespoon olive oil, 1 teaspoon salt, and a pinch of black pepper in a bowl. Toss to coat. Transfer the mixture to a baking pan, and roast for 10 minutes. Add three-quarters of the sliced shallots, and return to the oven. Cook until tender and golden brown, 20 to 30 minutes.
2. Combine sugar, cinnamon, cayenne pepper, and ½ teaspoon salt in a small bowl. Place the pumpkin seeds on a baking tray, and roast for 3 to 5 minutes, until the seeds begin to pop. Remove from oven, and transfer to a bowl. Drizzle with honey, and toss to coat. Sprinkle spice mixture over the seeds, and toss to coat. If they still seem sticky, let them cool, spread in a single layer, on a baking sheet.
3. Finely mince the remaining sliced shallots, and place in a large bowl. Add the balsamic vinegar, remaining ½ teaspoon of salt, and a pinch of pepper; whisk to combine. Continue whisking, slowly drizzling in the remaining 3 tablespoons olive oil. Add the endive, lettuce, and the roasted squash, shallots, and pumpkin seeds; toss to combine.

LADIES' FINGERS

MAKES 4 DOZEN

The amount of flour you need will vary, depending on humidity. For Man Toes, form shorter, thicker digits, use plain almonds for toenails, and sprinkle with dried rosemary for knuckle hair.

    Red food coloring (optional)
24 blanched almonds, halved lengthwise
 2 cups warm water (110°F) plus 3 quarts plus 1 tablespoon
 1 tablespoon sugar
 1 scant tablespoon active dry yeast (one ¼-ounce package)
 5 to 6 cups all-purpose flour, plus more for work surface
 1 tablespoon coarse salt
 2 tablespoons baking soda
 1 large egg
    Sea salt
    Dried rosemary (optional)
    Vegetable-oil cooking spray

1. Place a small amount of food coloring, if using, in a shallow bowl, and, using a paintbrush, color the rounded side of each split almond; set aside to dry.

2. Pour 2 cups water into the bowl of an electric mixer fitted with the dough-hook attachment. Add the sugar; stir to dissolve. Sprinkle with the yeast, and let stand until the yeast begins to bubble, about 5 minutes.

3. In the bowl of an electric mixer fitted with the paddle attachment, beat 1 cup flour into yeast on low speed until combined. Beat in coarse salt; add 3½ cups flour, and beat until combined. Beat until dough pulls away from bowl, 1 to 2 minutes. Reduce speed to low; add ½ cup flour. Beat 1 minute more. If dough is sticky, add up to 1 cup more flour. Transfer to a lightly floured surface; knead until smooth, 1 minute.

4. Coat a large bowl with cooking spray. Transfer dough to bowl, turning dough to coat with oil. Cover with plastic wrap; let rest in a warm spot to rise until doubled in size, about 1 hour.

5. Preheat oven to 450°F. Heat 3 quarts water to a boil in a 6-quart straight-sided saucepan over high heat; reduce to a simmer. Add the baking soda. Lightly coat two baking sheets with cooking spray. Divide dough into quarters. Work with one quarter at a time, and cover remaining dough with plastic wrap. Divide first quarter into twelve pieces. On a lightly floured work surface, roll each piece back and forth with your palm into a long finger shape, about 3 to 4 inches. Pinch dough in two places to form knuckles. When all twelve fingers are formed, transfer to simmering water. Poach for 1 minute. Using a slotted spoon, transfer fingers to a baking sheet. Repeat with remaining dough, blanching each set of 12 fingers before making more.

6. Beat egg with 1 tablespoon water. Brush pretzel fingers with the egg wash. Using a sharp knife, lightly score each knuckle about three times. Sprinkle with sea salt and rosemary, if using. Position almond nails, pushing them into dough to attach. Bake until golden brown, 12 to 15 minutes. Let cool on a wire rack. Fingers are best eaten the same day; or store, covered, up to 2 days at room temperature.

B.A.T. SANDWITCHES

MAKES 6

A variation on the classic BLT, this sandwich uses arugula instead of lettuce.

 1 pound bacon
 1 loaf pullman or other white bread, sliced
 ½ cup mayonnaise
 2 bunches arugula, tough stems removed
 3 tomatoes, sliced

1. Preheat oven to 450°F. Arrange bacon on two baking sheets; bake until crisp, about 30 minutes. Remove from oven, and discard fat or reserve for another use. Set aside to cool.

2. Toast bread, and spread with mayonnaise. Layer with bacon, arugula, and tomato; top with second slice of bread.

A **STUBBIER VERSION** *of our pretzel Ladies' Fingers produces Man Toes, knuckles crusted with coarse salt and sprouting rosemary "hairs."*

crafty party

STENCILED CAKES

MAKES ONE 9-BY-13-INCH PAN AND ONE 8-BY-8-INCH
PAN OF GINGERBREAD, AND ONE 9-BY-13-INCH PAN
OF BROWNIES

*These cakes may be prepared using gingerbread and brownies,
or by using only one and doubling the recipe.*

FOR THE GINGERBREAD:

   1 cup boiling water
   2 teaspoons baking soda
2½ cups all-purpose flour
   1 heaping tablespoon ground ginger
   2 teaspoons ground cinnamon
  ½ teaspoon ground cloves
   2 teaspoons baking powder
   8 tablespoons (1 stick) unsalted butter, room temperature
  ¾ cup packed dark-brown sugar
   1 cup unsulfured molasses
   2 large eggs
   Vegetable-oil cooking spray

FOR THE BROWNIES:

   6 ounces unsweetened chocolate
12 tablespoons (1½ sticks) unsalted butter
   2 cups sugar
   3 large eggs
1½ teaspoons pure vanilla extract
   1 cup all-purpose flour, sifted
   Pinch of coarse salt
   *Sanding sugar (see the Guide), or mixture of half
   confectioners' sugar to half ground ginger, for sprinkling*

1. Preheat oven to 350°F. Lightly spray two 9-by-13-inch pans and an 8-by-8-inch pan with cooking spray. Line the bottoms with parchment paper, and set aside.

2. To make the gingerbread, combine water and baking soda, and set aside. In a large mixing bowl, sift together flour, ginger, cinnamon, cloves, and baking powder; set aside.

3. In another large bowl, cream butter. Add brown sugar; beat on medium-low speed until fluffy. Beat in molasses and baking-soda mixture until well combined. Beat in flour mixture on low speed until combined. Add eggs, and beat well.

4. Pour batter to equal heights in 9-by-13-inch pan and 8-by-8-inch pan. Bake 15 minutes; rotate the pans in oven. Bake 10 minutes more, or until a cake tester inserted into center comes out clean.

5. To make the brownies, melt the chocolate and butter in the top of a double boiler, or in a heat-proof bowl, set over a pan of simmering water; stir occasionally.

6. In an electric mixer fitted with the paddle attachment, beat the sugar and eggs on medium-low speed until fluffy, about 2 minutes. Add the melted-butter mixture. Beat on low speed until combined. Beat in the vanilla, then the flour and salt.

7. Pour the batter into 9-by-13-inch pan. Bake for 20 to 25 minutes or until a cake tester comes out mostly clean (there may be traces of brownie if still moist); do not overbake.

8. Let the gingerbread and brownies stand on a wire rack until cool enough to unmold, 20 to 30 minutes. Unmold onto a clean piece of parchment paper, flipping over so they cool with top sides down and parchment-lined sides facing up. Carefully peel off parchment paper as soon as possible, while they are still slightly warm, so the surfaces are smooth for stenciling; let cool completely. (May be made a day ahead up to this point, tightly wrapped, and stored at room temperature.) Use square and round cookie cutters to cut out shapes. Place a stencil on a shape, and carefully sprinkle sanding sugar or confectioners' sugar mixture over stencil. Remove stencil. Transfer cakes to serving platter. Repeat until all the gingerbread and brownies are used.

templates

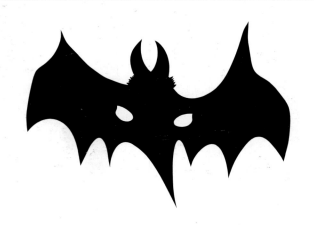

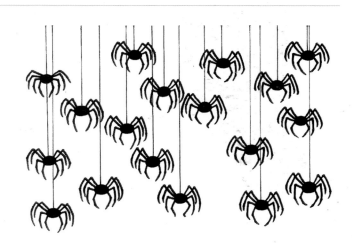

lighting the night

PAGE 14 PUMPKIN AND SQUASH SEED VARIETIES, *from The Cook's Garden, 800-457-9703 or www.cooksgarden.com; Harris Seeds/Garden Trends, 800-544-7938; Park Seed Company, 1 Parkton Avenue, Greenwood, SC 29647, 803-845-3369; Johnny's Selected Seeds, Foss Hill Road, Route 1, Box 2580, Albion, ME 04910, 207-437-9294; Seed Savers Exchanges, 3076 North Winn Road, Decorah, IA 52101, 319-382-5990 (seeds available on a trade basis); and Shepherd's Garden Seeds, 30 Irene Street, Torrington, CT 06790, 860-482-3638 or www.shepherdseeds.com.* **PAGE 17** Japanese KEYHOLE SAW (#49108.01), $15.95, *from Garrett Wade Catalog; 800-221-2942 or www.garrettwade.com.* Large PLASTER SCRAPER, $9; 1³/4-inch FLESHING TOOL, $3.40; X-Acto #15 SAW BLADE, $5.40 for 2; X-Acto #2 medium-weight UTILITY-KNIFE HANDLE, $3.16; and X-Acto #6 heavy-duty contoured ALUMINUM KNIFE HANDLE, $6.80, *from Pearl Paint, 308 Canal Street, New York, NY 10013; 212-431-7932 or 800-221-6845.* **PAGES 17–29** Ultimate PUMPKIN-CARVING KIT (CPC001; includes keyhole saw, scraper, hole cutters, melon baller, needle tool, linoleum cutter, and battery-operated mini-lights), $75, *from Martha by Mail; 800-950-7130 or www.marthastewart.com.* **PAGE 18** 7/8-inch HOLE CUTTER, $3.99, and ¹/2-inch HOLE CUTTER, $2.39, *from Pearl Paint; see above.* 2-inch star COOKIE CUTTER, $2.99, and Ateco 12-piece assorted JELLY-CUTTER SET (#4848), $12.99, *from New York Cake & Baking Distributor, 56 West 22nd Street, New York, NY 10010; 212-675-2253, 800-942-2539, or www.nycakesupplies.com. $10 minimum phone order.* **PAGES 22–23** DOUBLE-ENDED SCULPTING TOOL by Sculpture House, $7.20; X-Acto #6 UTILITY KNIFE, $6.80; and 3-inch BLADES, $2.20 for 5, *from Pearl Paint; see above.* **PAGE 27** 6⁵/8-inch NEEDLE TOOL (PRO), $1.51; SABER SAW (SBR), $1.35; HOLE CUTTER, $7; and #1 Speedball LINOLEUM CUTTER (#41231), $7.60, *from Pearl Paint; see above.*

conjuring a glow

PAGE 30 20-gauge annealed IRON WIRE (IR4773), $7.35 per 2-lb. spool, *from Metalliferous, 34 West 46th Street, New York, NY 10036; 212-944-0909.* Assorted WOOD SCULPTOR'S GOUGES, $17.10 to $36, and large PLASTER SCRAPER, $9, *from Pearl Paint, 308 Canal Street, New York, NY 10013; 212-431-7932 or 800-221-6845.* **PAGE 33** AMBULONG NUTS in bowl, $10 for bag of 20, *from Dry Nature Design, 129 West 28th Street, New York, NY 10011; 212-695-8911. $6 charge for shipping.* **PAGE 34** CANDLE WICKING, $1.60 per pack, and WICK HOLDER TABS, $1.60 per pack of 20,

both by Walnut Hill, *from Pearl Paint; see above.* **PAGES 34–41** Ultimate PUMPKIN-CARVING KIT (CPC001), $75, *from Martha by Mail; 800-950-7130 or www.marthastewart.com.* **PAGE 35** Japanese KEYHOLE SAW (#49108.01), $15.95, *from Garrett Wade Catalog; 800-221-2942 or www.garrettwade.com. Free catalog.* 1³/4-inch FLESHING TOOL, $3.19, *from Pearl Paint; see above.* PARTY LIGHTS, $20 for string of 10, *from Just Bulbs, 936 Broadway, New York, NY 10010; 212-228-7820 or www.justbulbs.com.* **PAGE 36** Assorted WOOD SCULPTOR'S GOUGES, $17.10 to $36, and 1³/4-inch FLESHING TOOL, $3.19, *from Pearl Paint; see above.* **PAGE 37** French 1930s MIRROR, *from Reymer-Jourdan Antiques, 29 East 10th Street, New York, NY 10003; 212-674-4470.* **PAGE 38** Speedball LINOLEUM HANDLE, $3.40; wide- and medium-line CUTTERS, $1.99 for 2; 6⁵/8-inch NEEDLE TOOL (PRO), $1.51; #1 Speedball LINOLEUM CUTTER (#41231), $7.60; and MEDIUM GOUGE #2 (L333-62), $6.14, *from Pearl Paint; see above.* **PAGE 39** TWINE, $8.50 per 100-yard spool, *from The Caning Shop; 800-544-3373.* Assorted WOOD SCULPTOR'S GOUGES, $17.10 to $36; PLASTER SCRAPER, $9; and 1³/4-inch FLESHING TOOL, $3.19, *from Pearl Paint; see above.* **PAGES 40–41** Brass BALL CHAIN (BRA824), $3.60 per 10 feet; brass COUPLINGS for ball chain (BRA836), 80¢ for 10; and 25-gauge ANNEALED IRON WIRE (IR4760), $4.70 per 80-oz. spool, *from Metalliferous; see above.* **PAGE 42** Cromatica WHITE VELLUM, $1.80 per 25-inch-by-38-inch sheet, *from Pearl Paint; see above.* **PAGE 43** Circus CANDY STICKS, *from Kencraft; www.kencraftinc.com.* Translucent white PAPER SHADE, $27 to $44, *from Just Shades, 21 Spring Street, New York, NY 10012; 212-966-2757.* **PAGE 44** 28-inch-by-40-inch German TISSUE PAPER in ocher, orange, and dark brown, $2.50 per sheet, and 24-inch-by-36-inch lightweight Nomex HEAT-RESISTANT PAPER, $7.50 per sheet, *from Kate's Paperie; 888-941-9169.* Nonadhesive LAMPSHADE STYRENE, $8.40 per yard, *from The Lamp Shop, 8 McGuire Street, Concord, NH 03301; 603-224-1603.* **PAGE 45** Assorted glass-cylinder VASES, $5 to $35 each, *from Kervar, 119 West 28th Street, New York, NY 10001; 212-564-2525.*

trading faces

PAGES 46, 52–57, AND 62–67 Ben Nye SPIRIT GUM, $4 per 1-oz. bottle; Stein's SPIRIT-GUM REMOVER, $2.75 for 4 oz.; RCMA NO-COLOR POWDER, $5.95 for 3 oz.; LATEX WEDGES, $2.99 for block of 8; and large POWDER PUFF, $1.50, *from Alcone Company Inc.; 800-466-7446 or www.alconeco.com. Free catalog.* **PAGES 46 AND 52–53** Kryolan EYEBROW PLASTIC, $6.50;

Ben Nye CREAM COLOR LINER in CL-1 white and CL-29 black, $3.75 each; FALSE EYELASHES, $2.50 to $5.50; and Duo EYELASH ADHESIVE, $5; *from Alcone Company Inc.; see above.* **PAGES 48–51 AND 58–59** Gylcerin-preserved OAK LEAVES, *available seasonally from Frontier Flowers, Route 1, Box 28B, Lakin, KS 67860; 316-355-6177.* LEMON LEAVES, yellow and red OAK LEAVES, and dried BLEACHED FERNS, *from O.K.S. Flowers, 123 West 28th Street, New York, NY 10001; 212-268-7231.* FEATHERS, *from Dersh Feathers Trading, 62 West 36th Street, New York, NY 10018; 212-714-2806. To the trade only.* **PAGE 50** BRIDAL CAP, *available at bridal stores.* **PAGES 54–55** Ben Nye PRESSED EYE SHADOW, $5; Woochie BALD CAP, $9.50; Kryolan EYEBROW PLASTIC, $6.50; Ben Nye CREAM COLOR LINER in CL-1 white and CL-29 black, $3.75 each; and Ben Nye pressed EYE SHADOW, $5, *from Alcone Company Inc.; see above.* **PAGES 56–57** Kryolan super-color ALL-COLOR PALETTE, $60, and Ben Nye plains DUST POWDER, $7.50 for 4.5 oz., *from Alcone Company Inc.; see above.* **PAGES 62–63** Woochie foam CAT FACE, $7, and Kryolan super-color ALL-COLOR PALETTE, $60, *from Alcone Company Inc.; see above.* **PAGES 64–65** STEIN DERMAWAX, $3.30; Ben Nye cuts and bruises GREASEPAINT WHEEL, $9; Ben Nye FRESH SCAB, $4.75; Kryolan black STIPPLE SPONGE, $1.80; Kryolan TOOTH ENAMEL in black, $6.10; and Ben Nye THICK BLOOD, $4.75 for 1 oz., *from Alcone Company Inc.; see above.* **PAGES 66–67** Woochie SPACE EARS, $9; CREPE HAIR, $5 per yard; Kryolan super-color ALL-COLOR PALETTE, $60; scarecrow DELUXE FANGS, $15; and Kryolan color HAIRSPRAY, $5.75, *from Alcone Company Inc.; see above.*

haunting a house

PAGE 70 Waxed-linen TWINE, $8.50 per 100-yard spool, *from The Caning Shop; 800-544-3373.* **PAGE 71** Vintage embossed VELVET LEAVES, $2 for small, $3 for large, *from Christina Lane; 845-358-3256. By appointment only.* Black paper PARASOL, $3.95 to $10.15, *from Pearl River Mart, 277 Canal Street, New York, NY 10013; 212-431-4770.* **PAGES 72–73** Sheer CHIFFON, *available at fabrics stores.*

pumpkin-carving feast

PAGES 83–93 Pennsylvania HARVEST TABLE and reproduction redware VASES, *from James Kieran Pine, 251 Pantigo Road, East Hampton, NY 11937; 631-907-1018.* Oxblood DINNER PLATES, $25, *from Global Table, 107–109 Sullivan Street, New York, NY 10012; 212-431-5839.* Canvas APRON (#961-1020), *from Janlynn Corp.; 800-445-5565.* Ultimate PUMPKIN-CARVING KIT (CPC001), $75, *from Martha by Mail; 800-950-7130 or www.marthastewart.com.* 6⅝-inch NEEDLE TOOL (PRO), $1.51; MEDIUM GOUGE #2 (L333-62), $6.14; PLASTER SCRAPER (#90A), $13.50; SABER SAW

(SBR), $1.35; HOLE CUTTER (HC1A), $1.91; and #1 Speedball LINOLEUM CUTTER (#41231), $7.60, *from Pearl Paint, 308 Canal Street, New York, NY 10013; 212-431-7932 or 800-221-6845.*

ghoulish supper

PAGE 98 White PORCELAIN BOWL, $37, *from Global Table; 107–109 Sullivan Street, New York, NY 10012; 212-431-5839.* **PAGE 100** Hakoutoun PLATE, *from Global Table; see above.*

crafty party

PAGE 107 Cat or owl HALLOWEEN LOOT PAIL, $15 for 3 qts. (DCB001) or $18 for 5 qts. (DCB002), and PARTY PLACE SETTINGS of tablecloth, napkins, plates, cups, place mats, and plastic utensils (XPS002), $26, *from Martha by Mail; 800-950-7130 or www.marthastewart.com.* 3M Command adhesive POSTER STRIPS, *from 3M; 888-364-3577.* **PAGE 108** Laser-print POSTCARDS, $20.90 for 200, *from Paper Access; 800-727-3701.* **PAGE 110** 30-inch rice-paper GLOBE, $19, *from Pearl River Mart, 277 Canal Street, New York, NY 10013; 212-431-4770.* **PAGES 118–119** Glassine-lined black CAKE BAGS, *from Krepe-Kraft, 4199 Bayview Road, Blasdell, NY 14219; 716-826-7086 for locations.* PAPER BAGS (#4065009), $3.95 for 28, *from Sax Arts & Crafts Catalog; 800-558-6696. Minimum order $10.* PINKING SHEARS, *from Fiskars, 7811 West Stewart Avenue, Wausau, WI 54401; 715-842-2091 or www.fiskars.com.* **PAGES 120–123** Nylon turtleneck LEOTARD (#6312), $25, and nylon TIGHTS (#51), $4.20, *from Danskin; 800-288-6749.* FLORAL TAPE, $1.99, *from New York Cake & Baking Distributor, 56 West 22nd Street, New York, NY 10010; 212-675-2253, 800-942-2539, or www.nycakesupplies.com. $10 minimum phone order.* Thread-covered FLORAL WIRE, *available from craft- and floral-supply stores nationwide.*

wickedly good menus

PAGES 125–134 Sugar PUMPKINS (available in October and November), *from Indian Rock Produce; 800-882-0512.* WALNUT OIL, $17 per bottle, *from Zingerman's; 888-636-8162.* DRIED CRANBERRIES, $4.50 for 6 oz., *from American Spoon Foods; 800-222-5886.* SILPAT BAKING MAT (KSP001), $38, *from Martha by Mail; 800-950-7130 or www.marthastewart.com.* GOLDEN SYRUP, $2.75, *from King Arthur Flour Baker's Catalogue; 800-827-6836 or www.kingarthurflour.com.* FLORAL TAPE, $1.99; FOOD COLORING, $2.99 per bottle; and orange SANDING SUGAR, $1.99 for 4 oz., *from New York Cake & Baking Distributor, 56 West 22nd Street, New York, NY 10010; 212-675-2253, 800-942-2539, or www.nycakesupplies.com.* BRANSTON PICKLE, $3.76 for 9 oz., *from British Traditionals; 803-505-6500 or www.britishtraditionals.com.*

WILLIAM ABRANOWICZ
16, 17 *(bottom right)*, 34 *(bottom)*, 35 *(top)*, 68, 70, 72 *(top left and right)*, 73, 75, 76 *(bottom right)*, 77

ANTHONY AMOS
24

SANG AN
97–101, 116, 117, 131, 132

CHRISTOPHER BAKER
12, 104

DIANA BRYAN
135–36

REED DAVIS
26, 44 *(all but bottom right)*

JOHN DUGDALE
15

DANA GALLAGHER
79, 96, 102, 103 *(top right)*, 108 *(top right)*, 133

GENTL & HYERS
Cover *(all but top left)*, 6, 7, 11, 28, 29, 48–51, 58–61, 71, 72 *(center and bottom right)*, 74, 76 *(all but bottom right)*, 78, 81, 94, 103 *(left row)*, 107, 109 *(top left)*, 110, 111 *(bottom right)*, 112–13, 114 *(top)*, 118, 120 *(bottom right)*, 122 *(top left)*, 123, 124, 138

GRACE HUANG
44 *(bottom right)*, 45

LISA HUBBARD
30, 35 *(all but top)*, 36, 38 *(top three)*, 39–41

STEPHEN LEWIS
114 *(bottom right)*, 115, 119

VICTORIA PEARSON
Cover *(top left)*, 18 *(top)*, 19, 22, 23, 25

DAVID PRINCE
4, 17 *(all but bottom right)*, 18 *(all but top)*, 21 *(all but bottom)*, 88 *(bottom left)*

DAVID SAWYER
33, 34 *(all but bottom)*

VICTOR SCHRAGER
1, 5, 8, 14, 27, 37, 38 *(bottom three)*, 120 *(all but bottom right)*, 121, 122 *(all but top left)*

MATTHEW SEPTIMUS
108 *(all but top right)*, 109 *(all but top left)*, 111 *(all but bottom right)*, 114 *(bottom left)*

JENNIFER TZAR
46, 52–57, 62–67

SIMON WATSON
82–87, 88 *(all but bottom left)*, 89–93, 127, 128

ANNA WILLIAMS
20, 21 *(bottom)*, 42, 43

Art direction by Barbara de Wilde

Book design by Mary Jane Callister,
Brooke Hellewell, and Jenny Hoitt

Editor: Alice Gordon

Managing Editor: Shelley Berg

Text by Janine Nichols

Assistant Editor: Christine Moller

Copy Editor: Marc Bailes

Senior Design Production Associate: Duane Stapp

Design Production Associate: Laura Grady

SPECIAL THANKS TO ALL THOSE WHOSE INSIGHT, TALENT, AND DEDICATION
contributed to the creation of this volume, notably: Stephen Antonson, Roger Astudillo,
Celia Barbour, Brian Baytosh, Claudia Bruno, Kellyann Burns, Dora Braschi Cardinale,
Peter Colen, Amy Conway, Sue Corral, Cindy Di Prima, James Dunlinson, Stephen
Earle, Jamie Fedida, Amy Gropp Forbes, Stephanie Garcia, Lisa Germany, Melanio
Gomez, Kathleen Hackett, Robin Herrick, Joelle Hoverson, Eric Hutton, Brennan
Travis Kearney, Robert Kinnaman, Anjna Kirpilani, Jodi Levine, Peter K. Mars, Sophie
Mathoulin, Jim McKeever, Hannah Milman, Page Marchese Norman, Laura Nor-
mandin, Ayesha Patel, Eric A. Pike, George D. Planding, Lesley Porcelli, Debra
Puchalla, Paul M. Reeves, Margaret Roach, Kelli Ronci, Nikki Rooker, Scot Schy,
Strath Shepard, Lauren Podlach Stanich, Gael Towey, Alison Vanek, Laura Wallis,
Gregory Wegweiser, and Bunny Wong. Thanks also to Oxmoor House, Clarkson Potter,
Satellite Graphic Arts, Spectragraphics, and R. R. Donnelley and Sons. Finally, thank
you to Martha, whose enthusiasm for celebrating holidays inspires us all.